TO FREE OR FREEZE

that is the question

LEONARD E. READ

TO FREE OR FREEZE

that is the question

The Foundation for Economic Education, Inc.
Irvington-on-Hudson, New York 10533   1972

ABOUT THE PUBLISHER

The Foundation for Economic Education is a non-political, nonprofit, educational institution. Its senior staff and numerous writers are students as well as teachers of the free market, private ownership, limited government rationale. Sample copies of the Foundation's monthly study journal, *The Freeman*, are available on request.

Published May 1972

(paper) ISBN-0-910614-44-X
(cloth) ISBN-0-910614-45-8

To

The World's Most Important Person

CONTENTS

1 • HOW LOOSE THE TALK

Though his beginnings be but poor and low,
Thank God, a man can grow!
                                        —Florence Earle Coates

● How MUCH IS REALLY KNOWN about political economy, the principal subject of our concern? Many proclaim their expertise, but I have long contended that no one has more than scratched the surface.

Assume for the moment that my skepticism is warranted. In this case, the first step toward an improved understanding would be an acknowledgment of meager knowledge, for it is axiomatic that know-it-all-ness paralyzes the learning process. What could be worse, more self-defeating, than a massive ignorance of political economy mistaken for a first-rate knowledge!

Is there, perhaps, a yardstick that can be used to gauge in a rough sort of way the understanding that attends a particular subject, discipline, specialization? Reflect on this: In those matters where opinions vary wildly and many persons presume to speak authoritatively—each claiming the last word—proficiency is at a minimum. This is to suggest that we can estimate how limited the knowledge by observing how loose the talk.

Few of us venture authoritative opinions about astronomy, atomic energy, computer design, crude oil refinement, metallurgy, hybridization, aerodynamics, electronics, voice transmission, pasteurization, combustion, and countless other specializations. We may infer that there is indeed expertise in these areas because there is a minimum of loose talk; most of us know we do not know.

Now shift to a subject on which there is much loose talk, many speaking as experts: cures for physical and mental ills. We hold strong, diverse opinions as to what kills and what saves. It is my guess that more than 99 per cent of all therapy is administered by other than professional practitioners—everything from midwifery, to home remedies, to countless patent medicines, to voodoo. The list is endless. While there have been striking advances in the various types of therapy, the professionals in this field have been changing their minds ever since Hippocrates. And the few who have my confidence are those who confess to knowing very little about Creation's miraculous human being.

Individual human therapy is one problem; social therapy is that problem compounded. Yet, in what other area can one find so many "experts," so much dogmatism, the loose talk so flagrant? Leave aside every Tom, Dick, and Harry who thinks he has all the answers, and consider the professionals—sociologists, economists, political scientists; they are at sixes and sevens. In no other field is there such a babble of tongues. So, according to my yardstick, the subject of political economy is to be approached only after a confession of minuscule knowledge, a frank acknowledgment that we have little more than scratched the surface.

Inasmuch as an M.D. knows very little about any individual, including himself, it seems improbable that any person knows very much about millions of diverse, varied persons, all unlike and unequal in every significant respect. Thus it is that all attempts at a planned society, be they for two dozen or two hundred million persons, fall in the category of pipe dreams. Man can no more plan the good society than he can intelligently plan the life of another human being. How can anyone logically expect to shape the lives of others beneficially when, in all honesty, the shaping of one's own life is so far from perfection! In other words, one's very willingness to manage society should be proof enough that he is unqualified.

Where then does this leave us? What recourse do we have? There is one unequivocal answer and only one: freedom! That is, allow everyone to go his own way, whatever it is, so long as he does not infringe upon the lives of others. This is a nonprescriptive social philosophy, a way of life for all of us *and planned for all by not a single one of us:* Creation freely manifesting itself through each human being! As Karl Jaspers phrases it, "God works through the free decisions of individuals."[1]

Very well! Suppose we have agreed to reject all coercive social planning; now what do I mean by claiming that not

---

[1]See *Way To Wisdom* by Karl Jaspers (New Haven: Yale University Press, 1968), p. 72.

one of us has much more than scratched the surface? When we know enough to shun collective "solutions," what further knowledge do we need? My answer: we need a more adequate understanding of the case for freedom and a more competent means of explaining it. Actually, we never will really know freedom! The best we can do— and do not discount this—is to reach further and further in the direction of the unreachable.

> . . . we do not possess knowledge or wisdom—which is the end of philosophical inquiry; and moreover . . . not only do we not possess it at the moment . . . but . . . we *cannot* in fact have it . . . we are dealing with a perpetual "not yet."[2]

Man's Purpose Is to Grow

If this sounds discouraging, at least it is consonant with human destiny: we are here to grow, to gain in knowledge and wisdom; it is not expected that any of us is now or ever will be all-knowing, all-wise. Were we able to understand and explain how freedom works its wonders, we would, by the same token, be able to understand and explain Creation.

Would not freeing human energy, rather than freezing it, take us into some unpredictable wonderland? Yes, of course it would. In store for humanity would be a situation as un-imaginable to us as the American phenomenon would have been to cave dwellers. Who am I or anyone else to say

---

[2]See *Leisure the Basis of Culture* by Joseph Pieper. (New York: Pantheon Books, Inc., 1961), p. 142.

when or at what point evolution is to be arrested, Creation's wonders halted!

Here is the common fault: Being against socialism or the planned economy convinces most people that they have arrived; that there is no more to it; growing is no longer a requirement. Nothing better illustrates this shortsightedness than an experience here at FEE more than twenty years ago. In the early days we had only semi-monthly releases of small pamphlets—the *In Brief* series. It was suggested to me that we should slow up on our mailings because there were only two or three articles in the barrel and no new manuscripts in sight. In other words, we were nearing a productive dead end; what more is there to do! Even then I sensed that we had not scratched the surface in presenting the freedom philosophy, so we mailed what we had on hand as soon as possible. Not only has our barrel never emptied but ideas and manuscripts have flowed into it at a constantly accelerating rate!

Twenty some years ago we had a few books to recommend. We now have more than a hundred titles ranging all the way from Hazlitt's easy-to-read *Economics In One Lesson* to such profound tomes as Mises' *Human Action*. Even more impressive, we have in these intervening years presented close to 3,000 essays, with the quality improving annually.

True, from the ranks have emerged a few who stand head and shoulders above the rest of us, but I still insist that neither they nor we have more than scratched the surface! Nor will anyone ever—but each of us can grow!

To my personal experience: This is my sixteenth book, the ninth in the past eight years. The chapters which follow were written during 1971, a year, which on the surface, at least, witnessed the most rapid abandonment of the free society in American history. What possible good can come from this adversity? Is there not always something good in everything bad if we can but discern it? I side with the Roman, Horace, who wrote more than two thousand years ago:

> Adversity has the effect of eliciting talents which in prosperous circumstances would have lain dormant.

This trend toward socialism should have the effect of waking us, of stimulating the cortical faculties, instead of bringing resignation as it does in so many cases.

Let me share what may be the most important idea in this book. As I finished writing each of these 28 essays, I was barren of an idea for the next one. As far as I could see all was done—I stared into a void. But I have a faith, founded on experience, that if I keep staring—and wondering—then some idea in the seeming void will come to mind. And, so far, I have found no reason to change my faith. If growth be every man's destiny, then a solid faith in freedom will serve anyone.

* * *

Some of these chapters have appeared in our monthly study journal, *The Freeman,* or in *Notes from FEE,* and some have been elsewhere published or reprinted. Each was written as an essay, that is, independently and with no idea of combining them into a book. Yet, there is a central theme: freedom! And the purpose of this book is to share my latest attempts at scratching the surface.

2 • WHEN RATIONING COMES*

*We first make our habits, and then our habits
make us.
All habits gather, by unseen degrees,
As brooks make rivers, rivers run to seas.*
                                                        —Dryden

● PERHAPS THE MOST EFFECTIVE WAY to be-
gin a commentary on the rapidly deteriorating plight of
the individual in our society is to trace present policies to
their logical conclusion. For unless there be general awareness of the utter disaster that lies ahead, assuming no
change in direction, we will continue merrily along to a
complete loss of freedom. National doom, as some would
say, but, more important, I believe, self-destruction of the
individual.

The course we are on must lead inevitably to rationing!

Such a prognosis does not frighten many people these
days. Americans do not appear upset by the prospect, and

---

*This appeared in *The Freeman*, July, 1971. Subsequent events appear, so far, to confirm what must happen when embarked on a statist
course.

even the people most strictly rationed—doubtless the Russians, where the rule is to obey or lose your life—no more resent rationing than they regret the lack of automobiles. Why? These are conditions of life into which they were born and to which they have grown accustomed. Rationing is no more deplored by Russians than are speed limits by Americans.

Why are Americans so little disturbed by the threat of rationing? Partly because we have had so little experience with this type of repressive law, but mostly because rationing laws have rarely been obeyed or enforced here. There was some rationing during WW I and much more during WW II under OPA. Withal, we experienced little pain. Obedience, such as existed, was cushioned by the patriotic fervor that attends some wars. I repeat, rationing has worked slight hardship because it was never *made* "to work" in the U.S.A. As with all nonsensical law—prohibition, for instance—rationing has resulted in mass "underground" movements. Black markets thrived. And otherwise first-rate citizens by the millions became law breakers, schemers, liars, and looked upon their departures from rectitude with approval and humor—as an outguessing game!

Hidden Costs of Intervention

Painless, yes; costless, no! The long run cost would be far less had we obeyed and suffered the pain of these politico-economic outrages. Had we obeyed, we would now despise and fear rationing and would do all in our power to avoid a recurrence of this ultimate in authoritarianism. We chose the painless but costly course: a lowering of the ex-

emplary standards. Hardly any virtue—not even honesty—
remained sacred. And this is disastrous: to abandon everything sacred is to forego the possibilities of a society in
which individuals thrive best.

People who have no fear of rationing—the vast majority
—can be said to lack a politico-economic turn of mind. Obviously, such persons cannot relate what they do not understand to that which has not happened. Only a sharp
and shocking contrast could bring this horror acutely to
their appreciation.

Let us imagine an instant transplant of a typical American family from Omaha to Omsk—take them from where
they are and from what they are accustomed to and drop
them suddenly into that authoritarian situation of which
rationing is a logical and inevitable part. The first order of
business would be to secure food. Mother would have no
phone; but that would not matter, for there are no deliv-
eries. She is without a car to go shopping; cars are rationed to commissars and their aides. No taxies! So she walks
to a government store and lines up at the end of a queue.
At long last, it's her turn. What are the choices? She can
either accept or refuse the rationed items and in the quantities set by government. What a contrast from yesterday
in the U.S.A.! Mother, in that case, would understand what
rationing means. Shocking, to say the least.

No need to labor the point. Father would experience the
same thing, as would the children. For anyone who can
read the language of economic cause and effect, *rationing
is failure on parade!*

Why are most goods and services rationed in Russia?
Because the Russian economy is a failure; it is not produc-

tive. Why will goods and services be similarly rationed in the U.S.A. if we continue the present course? For precisely the same reason that the last barrel of water is rationed on a ship lost at sea: short supply, that is, not enough to go around. Socialism—the planned economy and welfare state —is woefully lacking in productivity; it results in scarcity. When we in the U.S.A. substitute socialism for free market practices to the extent the Russians have, our failure will match theirs; productivity will be no greater here than there. There won't be enough to go around.

The attempted rebuttal runs thus: Americans will no more heed rationing regulations in the future than they have in the past. No government can ever do this to us— we think! Such optimistic forecasting is naive. When the real crunch comes there will be no choice.

Americans could flout rationing in the past and get away with it because there was private ownership. Sugar or gasoline or whatever was always obtainable for some black market price. Such markets, however, presuppose something more than a barrel of water for a lot of thirsty people; they presuppose each having something of his own to trade!

When and if real scarcity obtains in our country, as in Russia, rationing will be *made* "to work." There will be no alternative except to abandon the entire socialistic rigmarole. Otherwise, any political hierarchy too tenderhearted to use the required violence to enforce rationing will be run out of office by those who are indifferent to human life. The worst, as Hayek says, will get to the top.[1] Given real scarcity, it has to be this way.

---

[1]See "Why the Worst Get on Top," in *The Road to Serfdom* by F. A. Hayek (Chicago: The University of Chicago Press, 1967), pp. 134-152.

Antecedents to Rationing

Why do people accept rationing? Those who envision its debilitating effect on individuals may wish to explore its antecedents in sequential order. For causes cannot be removed until they are known, which is to say that rationing is inevitable unless we know its derivation.

Rationing is the effect of a cause but that cause is the effect of a prior cause, and so on. What then is the cause that immediately precedes rationing? Scarcity, as already suggested!

Now, scarcity is one of the facts of nature, in the sense that life is always a struggle. Largely by trial and error, some men at some times and in some parts of the globe have hit upon specialization and trade, voluntary cooperation in market fashion, to make the best possible use of scarce resources. In other words, they have developed the principles and practices of private ownership and free trade, with government limited to keeping the peace—no man-concocted restraints against the release of creative energy: freedom!

But not all men subjected to the competition of the market are content with the results. And their efforts to bypass the market, or do away with it, result inevitably in what I would call a contrived scarcity. This is what we witness in Russia and will experience here short of a turnabout. This kind of scarcity emerges from coercive interventions in the market: state ownership and control of the *means* as well as the *results* of production. Socialism!

Contrived scarcity, the cause of rationing, is itself an effect of still another cause. What is *its* immediate antecedent, that is, what are the components of coercive intervention? Wage, price, production, and exchange controls!

A few samples will suffice to make my point. Import embargoes and their variants, quotas and tariffs, make for scarcity. Impose embargoes on all exchange, domestic as well as foreign, and everyone, except the few who could survive by foraging, would perish. Contrived scarcity!

Minimum wage laws and arbitrary labor union wage rates make for unemployment and, thus, lower production. More contrived scarcity!

Paying farmers not to farm is an instance of production control—a political contribution to scarcity.

Medicare, where government, not the patients, pay the ever-increasing prices, is already making for a scarcity of hospital beds and, as socialized medicine progresses, there will be a scarcity of doctors.[2]

These and countless other political interventions are a form of price control—contrived scarcity driving prices upward. Sooner or later, as this trend becomes intolerable, government will "come to the rescue" with the opposite and generally accepted concept of price controls—limiting prices, that is, holding them down. Rent control falls in this latter category. Merely observe, whether such controls are invoked in France, Sweden, or New York City, that a housing scarcity follows.[3]

This form of price control can no longer be taken lightly.

---

[2]See "Why I Left England" by Dr. Edward L. McNeil. *The Freeman*, May, 1971.

[3]For an enlightening study of rent control and its effects in France, see "No Vacancies" by Bertrand de Jouvenel, *Essays on Liberty*, Vol. 1, p. 146. (Irvington-on-Hudson, N.Y.: The Foundation for Economic Education, Inc., 1952), p. 146.

Congress has given the President powers to invoke these counteracting controls at his discretion. Already, threats of such imposition have been directed at certain "key" industries. As prices continue to soar, we can expect the application of controls to all aspects of the economy. So long as present trends prevail, there is no political alternative.

Controls are invoked to cope with the constantly rising prices of which consumers complain. What, it may be asked, brings on these inordinate prices? Seeking the cause which is pushing all prices upward we come to the next antecedent, *inflation*.

Inflation is a *dilution* of the medium of exchange, an artificial expansion of the money supply. Inflation differs from counterfeiting in that it is legal and, also, it is an act of government rather than of individuals. But whether the money results from inflation or from counterfeiting, a dollar is a purchase order, and no one inquires into its source. A transaction involving counterfeit or inflation dollars is not an exchange of goods and services for goods and services but an exchange of paper money for goods and services. As the volume of paper money increases and as the quantity of goods and services decreases, everything else being equal, prices correspondingly rise. The equation is simple: Assume goods and services to be what they are now. Double the amount of money and prices will be twice as high.

However, inflation itself is the effect of a cause. What is *its* antecedent? The answer: excessive governmental expenditures!

Whenever governmental expenditures rise beyond the point where it is no longer politically expedient to defray them by direct tax levies, governments have only two choices: (1) go into nonrepayable debt or (2) inflate the money supply. The latter, a means of siphoning personal savings into the coffers of government, is the better political expedient because it is less understood and, thus, not so much opposed. Added to the billions collected by direct tax levies are these additional billions of expropriated private property. This is how overextended governments "balance" their budgets. Testimony to the general awareness that inflation depletes private savings is the attempt by millions of citizens "to hedge against inflation."

Who Drives Government Out of Bounds?

Overextended government is the weightiest of all the causes of scarcity for it lies at the very root of the formidable and dreaded rationing that looms ahead. Government doing the wrong things is the origin of all the aforementioned effects. Does out-of-bounds government, in turn, have a causal antecedent? If so, it cannot be stated with any more precision than a reference to the vagaries of human nature! Why is it that human beings behave as they do?

As this is written, I read of many distinguished men, reputedly free enterprisers to the core, who are pleading for Federal aid to bail out their ailing industry or community, or to compensate them for losses inflicted by droughts, or whatever. It seems that "private enterprisers" in trouble are, with few exceptions, as prone to turn to government as the socialists who revel in utopian dreams!

The tendency of those who say they favor private enterprise and related institutions is to blame socialists, communists, liberals, welfare staters, and the like for our deteriorating situation. Yet, when the chips are down and the going gets tough, the critics can hardly be distinguished from those they criticize. The former run to the Federal trough and turn the U.S.A. toward socialism as much as the latter. Such observations pronounce a harsh but humble verdict: we are well advised to look to ourselves as a major part of the problem. Why do we behave this way? Doubtless, there are more explanations than anyone knows, but here are a few suspected reasons.

The tendency to satisfy desires along the lines of least resistance, regardless of where such a course leads; in other words, a breakdown or failure of moral discipline.

An inability to reason from cause to consequence, from means to ends.

A failure to understand that government is essentially organized force, the uses of which are limited at best; in brief, no discernment as to what is or is not the appropriate role of government.

The naive assumption that government has funds of its own—a bottomless pot of gold—available for the asking.

The notion that feathering one's own nest at the expense of others is not robbery if it is legalized or has political santion.

The wishful thinking that others have a moral obligation to cover our mistakes and satisfy our wants; that wishes are rights.

A faith in socialism because the alternative is unknown, which is to say, an ignorance of the miracles that are wrought by men functioning freely in the market.

And then there is the tug of tradition, the heritage of political authoritarianism which with rare and brief exceptions, has featured human existence since the dawn of social organization. It is the ageless urge for security sought from a king; it is the reluctance to take the risks of self-responsibility, the refusal to become one's own man.

Perhaps there is nothing better we can do about the current dilemma than for each to openly acknowledge: "The fault is mine." For who among us adequately understands and can competently explain the freedom way of life we would uphold. No one!

I have tried here to pose the likelihood of rationing if we continue on the present course, and then to examine the cause of each effect—going backwards, so to speak, from where we now are. Admittedly, cause and effect are not always as precisely ordered as I have made them out to be; they are confusingly intertwined at times. But generally they follow in this sequence: (1) the vagaries of human nature ranging from "I want to be king" to "I want a king," (2) excessive government, (3) inflation, (4) controls, (5) scarcity, and (6) rationing with its stifling of individual growth and creativity, its smothering of the human spirit.

A recognition of where the present course leads should be enough to bring about a change in course, to do away with these numerous layers of intervention, to put government in its proper place, and to restore a reliance on the free market. Men free to produce and trade as they choose need not rely on rations for subsistence.

3 • TO EXECUTE A 180*

I feel and seek the light I cannot see.
— Coleridge

● WE WERE FLYING NORTH, destination Calgary. Near the Canadian border was an enormous "front." As our Captain ventured into it, the DC-6 bounced around as would a canoe on a storm-tossed sea. To go further would spell disaster, so the Captain executed a "180," returning to the airport from which we departed. Saved!

We are now headed into an economic "front." Wage, price, and other controls are a fact; they surround us. Unless we abandon these, rationing lies ahead and beyond that the total state—which spells disaster. How, in heaven's name, can we execute a "180"? What is the formula?

At the start, we must recognize that our wrong heading

---
*Pronounced one eighty, meaning a turn of 180 degrees, to reverse one's direction.

reflects a blind rejection of the free society. There is an abysmal lack of understanding of free market, private ownership, limited government concepts, imperatives, potentialities—not only among politicians but among leaders in business, the professions, and all walks of life. As actors who can recite the lines and the lyrics with ease, many repeat the words of freedom without the slightest inkling of their meaning. Mimics! The unlearned piloting the unwary!

There is but one cure for ignorance: enlightenment! Lesser treatments, such as "selling the masses," political activism, and the like, are an utter waste of time; as well try to bring daylight by cursing the darkness!

I have been claiming for years that enlightenment has precisely the same effect on ignorance as light has on darkness. Find out how to dispel darkness and we have a clue as to how the world may be rid of ignorance.

Darkness and ignorance have been used interchangeably since the dawn of language. So have light and enlightenment. "I am come a light into the world" meant an enlightenment, not a GE light bulb. What light does to darkness, enlightenment does to ignorance. These are comparable phenomena and we can save ourselves considerable frustration by recognizing this fact.

Let There Be Light

At a recent Seminar, I was demonstrating for the hundreth time that ours is a learning rather than a selling problem. The lecture room is reduced to inky darkness. In my hand is an electric candle controlled by a rheostat. The light is turned down to a mere speck. My explanation:

"Let me first call your attention to the fact that every eye is on this wee candle. (Obviously, for there is nothing else to see.) Here is my challenge: Increase the light in this room by selling, marketing, or distributing this speck of light. You will agree that it cannot be done. What purpose then can this wee light serve? Possibly, it may be sufficient for one nearby to find and light his own candle, in which case the light in this room would be increased 100 per cent. This could go on to the point where every one of you might find and light his own candle. There would then be enough light by which to read a book, even to write one.

"What I now wish to demonstrate is that darkness has no resistance whatsoever to light. Observe how it sneaks out of the room as light is increased. (The candle's light is gradually increased until at its brightest. Every face in the lecture room can be clearly seen—the darkness gone.) My point is that ignorance gives way to enlightenment precisely as darkness vanishes in the presence of light."

As I spoke those words—and thought about them—a devilish doubt flashed into mind: Can enlightenment possibly rid the world of the enormous ignorance we witness on every hand? Am I not exaggerating the power of enlightenment? I must confess that my faith faltered, if only for a moment. But that fleeting doubt had a lesson to teach me.

I realize now that the doubt grew out of my own egotism, a fantastic overassessment of self: the absurd notion that I and others like me possess an adequate enlightenment. Because ignorance is not giving way to our "brilliance," I began to suspect that enlightenment might not be the remedy for ignorance.

What, in fact, is my status? Just how brilliant am I? To what can my wisdom be compared? To that candle when its light is turned down to a mere speck! That's how brilliant I am—no more!

A Matter of Perspective

Look at this matter realistically. The tallest building on earth towers above its neighbors: the dock sheds on the Hudson. But compare their respective distances from the sun and the difference is negligible. Socrates stood head and shoulders above most men of his day or any other time; however, he took no note of the infinitesimal distinction between himself and the mill run of us. Rather, he compared the little he knew to the infinite unknown and declared, "I know nothing." The doubt that entered my mind for a moment is one that many others have found hard to shake. But it never bothered Socrates, for the simple reason that he assessed his own enlightenment in proper perspective. He was not distracted by his superiority over anyone else, because he was attracted by all there is to learn. His humble acknowledgment is the foundation of wisdom, and it points the way to such enlightenment as is within our powers.

Enlightenment alone is the remedy for all the ignorance there is. If we would judge how enlightened we are in the freedom philosophy, we need only observe how little is known of it. Perhaps you and I know more than the vast majority; but this is to proclaim that we know just a little more than nothing at all—faint praise, indeed! The fact is that no one of us has more than scratched the surface.

We who would execute "a 180" have in personal enlightenment the only rudder there is. And it depends on each of us whether he will use it to set himself on the right track.

The picture I have sketched is not as dismal as it first appears. Each of us who has done any homework at all can call to mind one person, or two, or perhaps several, who have made an about-face by reason of the minuscule understanding and expository qualities we have shared. We only need to step up our understanding—that's all!

Furthermore, the vast ignorance about the principles of freedom enhances such enlightenment as there is precisely as darkness makes visible the least glimmer of light. That tiny speck of light from the wee candle can and is seen in a dark room. Every eye is on it. Bear in mind that we seldom take note of the sun in broad daylight. The significance of this? In the vast void, in the current lack of understanding, our tiny enlightenments will stand out more than ever before. As wage and price controls and other authoritarian devices are inflicted upon us—as things go from bad to worse—be prepared for more attention, for others seeking an audience.

Merely make certain that the eye is on growth—increasing enlightenment—not on the audience!

4 • THE CRYSTAL BALL FANTASY

God will not suffer man to have a knowledge of things to come; for if he had prescience of his prosperity, he would be careless, and if understanding of his adversity, he would be despairing and senseless.

—Augustine

● I HAD BEEN severely critical of what's going on in our country. As the TV broadcast drew to a close, the interviewer asked, "Looking into your crystal ball, what do you see for the future?" My response: "I do not have a crystal ball and if I had one I could not read it—nor can anyone else!"

There is more than monetary inflation to plague us; there is also a flood of fortunetellers, soothsayers, tipsters, predictors, forecasters—those who attempt to size up the future by projecting present trends.

A noted physicist demonstrated the fallacy of this process: by extrapolating the increase in the number of scientists and of the total population in the first half of the twentieth century, we would, by the year 2000, have more scientists in the U.S.A. than people![1]

Imagine a predictor at the time of Christ. Observing the rate of increase in the number of pyramids during the previous 29 centuries, he predicted there would be X number in the year 1000. Suppose you had planned your construction industry on that kind of information! True, pyramid building continues even unto this day, but not of the Egyptian type. A pyramid is a monument to man's pride at the expense of others; the Taj Mahal is a pyramid, as is Brasilia, Venezuela's steel mill, the Gateway Arch, all Urban Renewal projects, and thousands of other economic monstrosities. But that ancient crystal ball gazer could not have forecast this change in the type of pyramids.

To gain an appreciation of how difficult it is to predict the future, merely observe how incompetent we are to report the past. No two historians agree; each sees the sketchy record through different peekholes. Try, for instance, to recall what you did last week and what went through your mind. Not very clear! But try to assess what went through your spouse's mind, or your neighbor's, or through the minds of millions unknown to you. Or their actions!

Even the record of current events is beclouded with misinformation. Public media reports are made by those whose sights may be no clearer than our own and are often bent to suit the reporter's bias.

[1]For two excellent articles on this point, see "The Year 2000 and All That," by Robert A. Nisbet, *Commentary*, June, 1968 and "The Theology of the Expotential Curve," by Gary North, *The Freeman*, May, 1970.

To what will the historian turn a thousand years hence to report on our times? *The New York Times*, perhaps? It is better indexed than other media! Much from this storehouse would be nothing more than reprintings of government handouts, hardly reliable data. And added to the inaccuracies of the source material will be the predilections of the various researchers. A distinguished historian explains why reporting the past is so varied and unreliable:

> What is it that leads one historian to make, out of all the possible true affirmations about the given event, certain affirmations and not others? Why, the purpose he has in his mind will determine that. And so the purpose he has in mind will determine the precise meaning which he derives from the event. The event, itself, the facts, do not say anything, do not impose any meaning. It is the historian who speaks, who imposes meaning.
>
> The historian has to judge the significance of the series of events from the one single performance, never to be repeated, and never, since the records are incomplete and imperfect, capable of being fully known or fully affirmed. Thus into the imagined facts and their meaning there enters the personal equation. The history of an event is never precisely the same thing to two different persons; and it is well known that every generation writes the same history in a new way, and puts upon it a new construction.[2]

I dwell on our difficulty in dealing with the past only to emphasize the impossibility of forecasting the "inevitable" future. Prediction that carries any meaning at all has to be modified by a great big "*If.*" For example:

---

[2]Professor Carl Becker, Cornell University, "What Are Historical Facts?" (1955) in Hans Meyerhoff (ed.), *The Philosophy of History in Our Time* (Garden City, N.Y.: Doubleday Anchor, 1959), pp. 131-132.

If our money supply continues to expand as it has for the past 32 years—from $31 billion to $225 billion—it will reach $1.4 trillion by the year 2000!

If governmental take-over of the economy and society continues in the future at the pace it has since adoption of the Sixteenth Amendment, the U.S.A. by the year 2000 will differ from Russia only in the words we use and the songs we sing.

Predictions—warnings, really—of this "if" variety could be expanded indefinitely. And this kind has a value: a challenge to correct the present. The past is prologue; the future's prologue is *now!*

As we cannot read the past with confidence, or the future at all, no one can tell what's in the making. We have but dim and shallow notions of what goes on in the minds of our contemporaries. For all anyone knows, the stage may be set for a complete turnabout during the next decade, or year, or month, or day. The law of action and reaction is always at work.

I once heard a golfer remark after sinking a 40-foot putt: "You have just witnessed a reaction to a perfect action." Moral? Look to our actions *now!*

5 • VOLUNTARY PARAMETERS

*With all our most holy illusions knocked
higher than Gilderoy's kite,
we have had a jolly good lesson, and it serves
us jolly well right!*

—Kipling

● MY OBJECT here is to examine and comment upon a statement made by the Secretary of the Treasury:

We are at the end of an era in our economic policy. It will be the disposition of the American people to have as few constraints as possible after the 90-day freeze period, and if we can get voluntary compliance now we can avoid stringent controls later. But it would be unwise to think we can go back to where we were before. American business and labor may have to get used to the idea of living within certain parameters."[1]

First, what is a parameter within which we may have to live? The simplest definition to be found in the dictionary:

---

[1] See *The New York Times*, August 29, 1971, p. 1.

. . . a quantity or constant whose value varies with the circumstances of its application, as the radius line of a group of concentric circles, which varies with the circle under consideration.

There are only a few in the whole nation who even know what parameters are, let alone how to live within them. Why the use of such a strange word? I suspect it is used for precisely the same reason that the Chairman of the Federal Reserve Board, some months earlier, borrowed and broadcast a British term, "incomes policy": to lessen the shock effect. The same applies to the more recent references to a "Stabilization Board."

To be open and above board about it, that is, to bluntly announce that we are in for wage and price controls and then rationing and that these mean an end to free market, private ownership practices would not set well with a substantial number of citizens. So, what is the political approach? To ease into the statism being prepared for us by employing terms so vague that hardly anyone knows what the intentions are. "Parameters" and "incomes policy" are perfect examples of this beating around the bush.

What are we to make of "voluntary compliance"? This is an absolute contradiction in terms. Put it this way: If you will not voluntarily jump out of the window, I shall take sterner measures to accomplish the same effect. Voluntary means something given or done by one's own free choice, the exercise of free will. Compliance means just the opposite: acquiescience or giving in.

In the days to come, this means that you yourself will either freeze wages and prices—regardless of supply and demand and what you would freely choose to do in the circumstances—or you will be compelled to do so. Respond to the threat of force, or down comes the force upon you! Voluntary, instead of meaning an exercise of one's own free will, turned around to mean that you are to behave according to somebody else's arbitrary will!

"We are at the end of an era in our economic policy." Most government officials believe we are, as do many businessmen, some columnists and so-called economists, and millions of others. Perhaps we are! But this verdict should not be glossed over and accepted lightly.

First, note that the antecedents of the rationing to come are the wage and price controls presently imposed. The antecedent of these controls is inflation brought on by excessive governmental expenditures and money issue—and these, in turn, caused by millions of misguided people looking to government for security, welfare, and prosperity.

Second, note that current official pronouncements make no mention of the above sequence of causes or the need for removing them. This merely means that the welfare state and its concomitant, the planned economy, is accepted and assumed as a *fait accompli;* the new order is here—the total state! Buy this, and we are, indeed, at the end of an era. Russia, China, Cuba, and others have beat us to it, of course, in this century. But the history of price-fixing extends back at least 46 centuries in Egypt, China, Athens, Rome, Britain, India, the colonial experience in America, to mention a few—always with the same sad report: the end of an era.[2]

---

[2]See "Food Control During Forty-Six Centuries" by Mary G. Lacy in *Essays On Liberty,* Vol. 1, *op. cit.,* p. 229.

". . . it would be unwise to think we can go back to where we were before." Was it unwise for England, following the Napoleonic Wars, to abandon mercantilism by repealing three-fourths of some 18,000 laws restricting production, exhange, and pricing? There followed the greatest outburst of creative energy and mass well-being ever known up to that time. On the contrary, the restrictive laws under which England is again falling would seem to be what are most unwise.

True, the ideal free economy has never existed anywhere. The nearest approximation has been in the U.S.A. Wisdom suggests that we regain what we have lost, doing everything within our power to head off any move to the contrary.

Economics, the study of how to mitigate the effects of scarcity, concerns the search for answers to what should be produced and in what amounts and whose satisfactions are to be served. The free market, featuring open competition and free entry, has the consumer as king. Each decides what he wants, in what quantities, and at what prices, where he shall work, how many hours, and at what wage. With free, unrestricted pricing as the guidelines, the free market is always working toward a balance of supply and demand. The free market works automatically and "shortages" and "surpluses" are not in its lexicon.

Abandon the free market, and not the consumer but the politician becomes king. In the "new era," that king, rather than you and I, decides what shall be produced, what we shall have, in what quantities, and at what price. Can that be wise?

6 • THE QUICK FREEZE

Countries are well cultivated, not as they are fertile, but as they are free.

—Montesquieu

● APPROPRIATELY ENOUGH, the term "quick freeze" had its origin with a fishing experience. Nearly six decades ago, Clarence Birdseye, a young scientist, joined a fishing expedition to Labrador. He would pull his catch through a hole cut in the thick arctic ice, and in the sub-freezing air the fish were frozen before he could get them off the hook. Thawed and cooked weeks later, he discovered that there had been little loss in flavor or texture. Quick freeze, come upon quite inadvertently, was a new answer to the storage of numerous vegetables, meats, fish.[1]

Quick freeze is a technological step forward in the storage of eatables. But to freeze human endeavor—quickly or

---

[1]See "Food From Thought" by Charles W. Williams *(The Freeman,* November, 1968).

slowly, partially or completely—is a step backward from the production of things to be eaten. Storing food poses one set of problems, while coping with the scarcity of food—or clothes or shelter or whatever—poses another. These are not problems having similar solutions, even though some may treat them so.

The living fish is a mobile animal, wonderful to behold. Mobility—freedom of God-given faculties—is a prime feature of the ideal life be it fish or man. Freezing of either one is an act of immobilization. In the world of fish this is achieved by a drop in temperature, a death sentence; in the human world by a drop of the legislative hatchet, in effect, imprisonment. On August 15, 1971 a "freeze" was announced by the President of the United States. This really means, in spite of political jargon, a partial immobilization of the creative faculties—"We have had enough for the time being; stop here!"

The mobility of ideas and other forms of human energy is the very essence of their being. Creativity, on which all production depends, is a flowing, ever-moving force. It obeys its mobile nature or ceases to exist. But before creativity can be stopped altogether, it will turn to cheating, lying, law-breaking, and other forms of social error. Life and mobility are inseparable; to freeze the latter is to lessen the former.

Examples of Immobilization

If we contemplate the history of immobilization or freezing of human endeavor—a common tendency over the ages—the edict of August 15 should come as no surprise.

However, current examples will suffice for our point. Let us begin with a freeze that nearly everyone regards as contemptible; next, one that even highly "educated" people think commendable; finally, a few immobilizations that fall between the "awful" and the "good."

Recently, I made a round trip of 5,200 miles in one day for a business engagement. Mobility in dramatic form! A hundred people or so carrying out their aims peacefully. I did in a day what my grandfather could not have done in several months. Had our government imposed a "freeze" in his day, this mobility of mine would now be regarded as the figment of a flighty mind. But immobilization is upon us in a new form: hijacking! Talk about a quick freeze in the affairs of those thus victimized! What an immobilization of the free flowing of God-given faculties!

That's the "awful." Now for the "good": teacher tenure. This is an upper-class example of partial freezing—an out-and-out thwarting of mobility. Appointment as a teacher followed by a creditable performance for a brief period, and tenure is granted: "permanent possession, as of an office or position."

A job—teaching or whatever—is a realized opportunity. It is the merging of talents someone wants with talents someone else possesses. The talents wanted and those possessed are forever changing. Ideally, a job is an opportunity seized upon to the mutual advantage of employer and employee and should endure for the period their mutual interest is served, and no longer! Employer and employee are not mutually exclusive categories; indeed, each individual more often than not serves in both capacities at the same time: I work for someone else while there are those who work for me. In any event, the period of association should be determined by the duration of common interests, otherwise mobility is squelched.

The Urge for Security

Tenure amounts to immobilization, a partial freezing. When granted, a sign is hung on what otherwise would be an opportunity: "No vacancy." It has been granted or taken for life and, thus, is no longer an opportunity for others. Tenure is but another of countless devices aimed at a security which, in reality, is unobtainable. "There is no security on this earth," wisely observed Douglas Mac-Arthur, "there is only opportunity."

Look upon teaching or any other job for what it really is: a realized opportunity. Then attempt the mental gymnastic of fastening ownership on an opportunity. Might as well try to establish a personal proprietorship of "all this and heaven too." Impossible! Yet, this is precisely what labor unions attempt: they claim job ownership when they use violence or the threat thereof to keep others from taking the opportunities they have chosen to vacate. This, of course, is but the educational system's tenure proposition applied to labor union membership. This opportunity is mine, all mine! "Educators" showing unions the way! Immobilization on the grand scale! The freeze!

True, there should be equal opportunity for all—a fair field and no favor. But for anyone—a teacher or whoever—to claim an ownership of free access is grossly at odds with fact and logic. Ownership is control. And that which is owned by one is not available willy nilly to others. Ownership and free access are in two distinctly different conceptual categories.

When an employer controls an employee's life and energies, we quite properly refer to such control as slavery or bondage or servitude. *It is no less slavery when an employee or an association of employees denies an employer's freedom to associate with whom he chooses or otherwise restricts his exhanges for whom or for what he wishes.* It is just as immoral and uneconomic and anti-freedom for employees to freeze the God-given talents of employers as for employers to freeze the creativity of employees. There is not one whit of difference.

Protectionism Takes Many Forms

The propensity to immobilize creativity is not a weakness exclusive to labor unions and educational institutions. I cannot think of an occupational category that is exempt, be it medicine, architecture, the legal profession, engineering, banking, or whatever. It is as much in evidence in the business world as anywhere else. The tariff and all other forms of protectionism are nothing but ownership claims to exchanges. There is no distinction, none whatsoever, between the exchanges of services—jobs—and the exchanges of goods or things. The latter, as the former, when allowed, are but realized opportunities. As Bastiat wrote, freedom in transactions is an absolute principle. To inhibit this freedom, except in illicit traffic, is to deaden human mobility and thus to lessen life. It is to do to humanity what we do to fish—freeze!

All history fairly reeks with persons, groups, nations, often in violent and deadly combat, immobilizing the God-given faculties of competitors. The planned economy is the modern version of this ancient vice. In the final analysis, these efforts are a manifestation of envy,[2] an attempt at a pseudo-superiority; getting on top by holding others under; placement of oneself in the vanguard by the enforced retardation of other human beings! Competition and free entry are looked upon as evil things when, in fact, they are prime economic boons to mankind.

Denying Our Heritage

The most pronounced break with this bleak historical record occurred in the U.S.A. Here was an enlightenment that released creative human energy on a scale never before realized or since surpassed! But during the past six or seven decades, and at an ever-increasing pace, we Americans have been returning to an old-world mythology, a politico-economic medievalism. It seems that we have all but forgotten our own experiences. Most of us have learned little from history.

The freeze of August 15, and the subsequent "phases," with unbelievable applause and approval, is an up-to-date, clear-cut motion picture of the condition into which we are lapsing. To stop inflation is the excuse. However sincerely this fallacy is believed, the freezing of prices can only add to the woes inflation inflicts. Otherwise, price freezing is unrelated to inflation.

---

[2]For an excellent book on this, see *Envy* by Helmut Schoeck (New York: Harcourt, Brace, Javonovich, 1970).

Doubtless, the fallacy has its origin in thinking of inflation as a rise in prices. Inflation is, instead, a *dilution* of the money supply, nothing else. A rise in prices is one of the inevitable consequences of dilution. If by legislative fiat all prices were reduced to zero, the money supply would not be reduced one dollar. Price freezing is another of those utterly futile attempts to correct an evil by tampering with its effects. Like trying to remedy robbery by decreeing that the thefts amount to nothing—that no one is victimized!

In a highly specialized economy, exchanges depend on a circulating medium possessing integrity. Dilution of the medium—inflation—destroys the medium's integrity. When the medium becomes worthless, exchanges on which survival depends can be effected only by barter, a primitive device that can support no more than a primitive way of life. Try to exchange an airplane ride for so many geese or swap lectures for an automobile. Awkward!

While barter—direct exchanges without benefit of a circulating medium—is a primitive means of exchange, it may serve as the simplest way to grasp the full implications of a price freeze. For the sake of clarity, leave money aside; think only in barter prices.

Here is a sampling of barter prices: The price of a quart of milk is 1¼ lb. of squash, 2 cans of shrimp, 3 oz. of round steak ground, 1 oz. of shad roe, on and on for perhaps 10,000 items in a single supermarket. Going outside, the price of a quart of milk is one gallon of gas, two-thirds of the Sunday *New York Times*, 6 minutes of my secretary's time, one-sixth of a headlight bulb for my auto, a 3-minute phone call from Irvington, N.Y. to Irvington, N.J., on and on to millions of other items and literally trillions of exchanges.[3]

Merely bear in mind that each individual's desires are in constant flux and the same can be said for what he wishes to or can produce. Freeze prices as of this or any other moment, and to the extent that this effort succeeds, desires would be frozen as well as variations in productive temperament: creative energies slowed down, God-given faculties deadened.

What, in fact, are prices? Prices, whether in barter or dollar terms, are no more than voices announcing what you or I or others will give in exchange for this or that. To freeze prices, therefore, is to silence our voices.

Imagine that the head man of a controlled economy is the most brilliant ever to inhabit this earth, with every citizen of the U.S.A. devoutly committed to his every wish and whim—obedience to the letter. In this "ideal" situation all would perish!

This is not to advocate disobedience; it is, rather, to suggest that the freeze of human aspirations and endeavor— whether by government, unions, teachers, businesses, or anyone else—be abandoned. To immobilize man's creativity is both immoral and deadly.

---

[3]Lionel Robbins, chief economist of the British Government during WW II, has this to say about this kind of planning: "It would necessitate the drawing up of millions of equations on the basis of millions of statistical tables based on many more millions of computations. By the time the equations were solved, the information would have become obsolete and they would have to be calculated anew." See *The Great Depression* by Lionel Robbins (London: Macmillan, 1934), p. 151.

For an interesting study on this whole subject, see *Marx's Religion of Revolution* by Gary North (Nutley, N.J.: Craig Press, 1968), Appendix A.

7 • ADRIFT AND WITHOUT COMPASS

*The only freedom which deserves the name,
is that of pursuing our own good in our own
way, so long as we do not attempt to deprive
others of theirs, or impede their efforts to
obtain it.*

—John Stuart Mill

• I HAD STAKED OUT my subject matter and settled on the above title when a memorable event came to mind. Just 53 years ago today—February 5, 1918—the *Tuscania* was torpedoed and sunk in the Irish Sea. Lost were 213 men, but there were nearly 2,200 survivors. Why so many? Our troopship stayed afloat for three and one-half hours! Thirty of us were still aboard during her waning moments. Then, someone discovered a lifeboat on the poop deck which we managed to launch in a rough and frigid sea—adrift and without compass.

My thesis is that the U.S.A. is adrift and without compass. My hope is that we shall be spared some time and that we shall take advantage of this breathing space to find our bearings. This is possible if we know how to construct a compass.

But first, there has to be an awareness that we are adrift. This is easy enough to recognize in a lifeboat on a storm-tossed sea in inky darkness. One is quite aware of his plight. Not so in society! Few Americans, so far, appear to be conscious of what is wrong. People, by and large, have no awareness of lost freedoms. Like wild tigers, captured and put in zoos, they soon become docile and regard the what-is as the what-ought-to-be. Most Russians are not conscious of serfdom; rather, they enjoy their lot.

> My very chains and I grew friends,
> So much a long communion tends
> To make us what we are . . .[1]

Government Takes 43 Per Cent

A few can scan the decades, relate the freedoms which remain to the freedoms that no longer are, and infer we are adrift. But what about those who cannot or will not do this? How are they to gain an awareness of our plight? Will they understand and accept the statistical evidence? It is conceded that statistics are strikingly ineffective to awaken the lethargic. But let us consider a few simple facts.

The population of the U.S.A. in 1913 was 95 million; by 1970 the population had increased to 205 million.

Federal expenditures in 1913 were well under $1 billion; by 1970 they had increased to $210 billion!

In 1913 Federal expenditures amounted to less than $8

---

[1]From "The Prisoner of Chillon" by Lord Byron.

per person; by 1970 they averaged more than $1,000 per person—man, woman, child.

Stated another way, population in this period has slightly more than doubled; Federal expenditures are nearly 300 times what they were then.

However, it may not be fair to measure the growth of governmental take-over by Federal expenditures alone— for one thing, because of a deteriorating dollar. So, let us assess this trend by relating all governmental expenditures—Federal, state, local—to the people's earned income.

Bearing in mind that earned income has enormously increased in this period, total governmental expenditures equaled 9 per cent of earned income in 1913; by 1970 these expenditures had grown to 43 per cent of earned income. And the percentage continues to grow.

The rebuttal, by those of a socialist or interventionist persuasion, is founded on a confusion of cause and effect. In essence, it is this: If governmental take-over is destructive, how then are we to account for the enormous increase in earned income going hand-in-hand with the ever-increasing expansion of government spending, control, and ownership? The latter, according to the socialist view, obviously is responsible for the former; any fears of big government must be unfounded.

Two Directions at Once

There never has been an instance of progress without destructive forces going on simultaneously. "It has often been found that profuse expenditures, heavy taxation, absurd commercial restrictions, conflagrations, inundation, have not been able to destroy capital so fast as the exertions of private citizens have been able to create it."[2] However, would it not be folly to credit the progress to the destructive forces? The fact that they go on simultaneously may tell us something about the durable nature of man; but it doesn't prove that good ends result from evil or wrong means.

The truth of the matter, at least as I glean it: The free economy was more nearly approximated here than in any country at any time. This resulted in an unprecedented outburst of creative energy. The thrust of this was so great, producing a momentum of such force, economic muscle, and endurance, an economy of such wealth, that it has been able to support and withstand a parasitical growth of a magnitude never before known or possible. Parasites can proliferate only as the host grows in strength and increasingly supplies the sustenance on which they feed. But we should never infer that Marxist welfarism—"from each according to ability, to each according to need"—strengthens the host. Sooner or later, unless a compass is devised and used, there will be all parasites and no host!

If we are not already adrift, then I do not read the signs aright. The expenditures of government have for some years been too great to be met by direct tax levies. Capital assets are being confiscated—via inflation. Prices rise faster each year than income. Note what is happening to the railroads. The airlines are in an identical rut. Businesses by the thousands are in a bind. Individuals who lose their jobs in

---

[2]See *History of England* by Thomas B. Macaulay (New York: E. P. Dutton & Co.), Vol. 1, p. 217.

these cutbacks—private or governmental—have more and more difficulty finding other jobs. If socialism prevails, the next step is known: wage, price, production, and exchange controls, and then rationing—the total state! Freedom will remain in song and verse, but not in reality!

To summarize: We are adrift on a sea of socialism and without compass. Where are we to turn for an improved heading on this singularly rough and frigid sea? The forces that lead individuals, societies, civilizations this way or that are mostly over and beyond human design or intention. Choosing a course is far more complicated than we realize. Yet, there is a role for rationality, a reasonably simple comprehension, that is potentially within our reach. It is adequate, I hope, to steer us away from all-out statism and toward freedom. Nothing more pretentious than this is intended.

Excessive Government Is the Problem

Let us recognize at the outset that the basic problem of all-out statism is that of a government out of bounds, that is, government undertaking many tasks that are outside its principled scope. Such politico-economic retrogression results from an absence of intellectual underpinnings.

I am not suggesting that adequate intellectual underpinnings once existed and are now forgotten—only that we are retrogressing into socialism. Americans got off to a good start more inadvertently than by any rational design. Our forefathers came to this land that each might be his own man. True, they sought to insure freedom and self-responsibility through such political instruments as the

Constitution and the Bill of Rights. But they had no idea of the miracle that lay in store for their progeny. Further, they had no precise theory of what government should and should not do. If we can identify and set forth that sound theory of government it should provide the compass we need.[3]

The construction of our compass has to begin with a clear and precise understanding of the nature of government. Professor Woodrow Wilson, writing in 1900, gave us an exact answer: "Government, in its last analysis, is organized force."[4]

My explanation has been made many times but warrants repeating. The distinction between you as an agent of government and you as a private citizen is, that in the former role, you have the backing of a constabulary; issue an edict and we obey or take the consequences. Remove this backing and you are restored to private citizenship; issue an edict and we do as we please. Clearly, organized physical force is the essential, distinctive characteristic of government.

What can physical force or the threat thereof accomplish? What is within its power? It can only inhibit, restrain, penalize! And this is all government can accomplish.

This poses a logical question: What, in all good conscience, should be inhibited, restrained, penalized? The

---

[3]See "A Role for Rationality" in *Let Freedom Reign* (Irvington-on-Hudson, N.Y.: The Foundation for Economic Education, Inc., 1969), pp. 9-24.

[4]See *The State* by Woodrow Wilson (Boston: D.C. Heath & Co., 1900), p. 572.

answer is to be found in the moral codes: fraud, violence, misrepresentation, predation, that is, actions that do injury and injustice to others.

Bear in mind that the compass we seek, the course we would chart, is for the use or guidance of the individual in society. And note that the destructive actions to which we have referred—killing, stealing, lying, and the like—have to do with one's behavior toward others. One does not steal from himself, but from someone else; and so with killing, lying, or other acts of coercion. Acts of coercion occur in a social context, that is, the coercion one applies against another.

Government's Limited Role

We may infer from this that government—organized force—should be limited to preventing any of us from doing injury or injustice to others, that is, limited to keeping the peace—a fair field and no favors.

But note that this limited role of government does not include or condone the use of force to keep individuals from otherwise being themselves. Our compass is not intended to direct the life of any peaceful person, but only to enable individuals to live at peace and in harmony with one another. The only logical reason for inhibiting injury and injustice among men is to make possible for each of us to be himself and to surpass himself. To become our true selves is the destination, the objective we should have in mind.

Restraining pirates and marauders is but a means to that end. As a factory exists for the purpose of production, so man lives in order to evolve. And each worthy person or purpose deserves protection. But let not the guards take over either the factories or the lives they are to defend.

My belief is that all human progress is attributable to the creativity of individuals acting voluntarily. This is why I stress the importance of the freedom to be oneself, urge that this should be the objective or the destination for any society. And it seems to me that a government which inhibits destructive interferences in our lives is a useful means to that end: personal freedom. All the creativity there is springs from individuals being themselves. Creativity has selfhood as its source.

Creativity a Spiritual Force

If this conclusion requires any defense, here is mine. Physical force or the threat thereof—governmental or private—is definitely not a creative force nor can it ever be employed to induce creativity. Creativity is in all instances a spiritual force: the spirit of inquiry, invention, discovery, insight, intuition.

Ralph Waldo Trine phrased it thus:

Everything is first worked out in the unseen before it is manifested in the seen, in the ideal before it is realized in the real, in the spiritual before it shows forth in the material. The realm of the unseen is the realm of cause. The realm of the seen is the realm of effect. The nature of effect is always determined and conditioned by the nature of the cause.[5]

---

[5]From *In Tune With the Infinite* (Indianapolis: The Bobbs-Merrill Co., 1897).

And the eminent economist, Ludwig von Mises, has this to say:

> Production is a spiritual, intellectual, and ideological phenomenon. It is the method that man, directed by reason, employs for the best possible removal of uneasiness. What distinguishes our conditions from those of our ancestors who lived one thousand or twenty thousand years ago is not something material but something spiritual. The material changes are the outcome of spiritual changes.[6]

Whatever shows forth of a spiritual nature emanates from discrete individuals. Society discovers or invents nothing. Insight is not a group process but a singularly personal phenomenon. And it cannot be induced or hastened by coercive force.

The harm or good an individual does to self is not only beyond the power of physical force to regulate but all would-be regulators are absolutely blind to what goes on within you and me. In the first place, this is none of their business and, second, all attempts at using such force to adjust the human psyche must result in mischief. It is bound to deaden creativity, and in no way—none whatsoever—can it correct or improve moral judgments.

How you mind your own business, whether to downgrade or upgrade yourself, is strictly a private affair. To regard you, in this sense, as a social or governmental responsibility, is to miss the point entirely. This confused view of authority and responsibility largely accounts for our being adrift.

---

[6]See *Human Action* (Chicago: Henry Regnery Company, Third Revised Edition, 1966), p. 142.

It is one thing to construct a compass for the ship of state, to steer a course of limited government. But such a compass will not and cannot give appropriate readings for the peaceful and creative activities of individuals. To thus confuse the purpose of the societal compass is to steer away from freedom and set ourselves adrift in a sea of socialism.

What one does to himself or with his own life is not the business of society or within the province of organized force. This would be an artificial and incorrectly deduced relationship. The true relationship, in this respect, is between a man and his God and/or his conscience.

The compass that can steer us aright is simple. Merely limit government to the only role it can usefully play, namely, inhibiting injuries and injustices which some persons or groups may try to inflict on others. No special privileges for anyone; no coercive parasitism, thus permitting each to be his creative self.

8 • LOOKING IN THE MIRROR

Though the enemy seem a mouse, yet watch him like a lion.

—Proverb

● IT HAS BEEN SAID that there is something wrong with any action or behavior that is not joyous; ". . . life must be felt as a joy," wrote Albert Jay Nock. At first blush, this appears to be a partial truth at best, for are not some actions devoid of joy? Take criticism, for instance. Criticizing others may give the critic a perverse level of satisfaction, but self-criticism is rarely attended with pleasure. In this circumstance, joyousness as a criterion seems to rule out self-criticism. But once a person realizes that seeing and remedying his own faults is far more rewarding than carping at others—that it is vital to personal growth—then self-analysis and self-criticism can be a joyous undertaking.

Holding my own work up to the mirror of self-criticism reveals a now-and-then unfortunate result which should be examined for some personal omission or fault. Something, it seems, has been missing in my presentations of the freedom philosophy.

Were you a teacher of astronomy and some of your listeners or readers became astrologists, or of chemistry and a few turned to alchemy, you would look to your teaching. My problem, and doubtless that of others, is of this sort.

Over the past several decades countless individuals who had been only vaguely familiar with the freedom philosophy have told me that my lectures and writings have "turned them on." They concede to having been liberated from apathy into a state of devoted concern and interest. So far, so good; indeed, all to the good.

Now, I would be the first to admit that speculations of the most diverse and contradictory sort have gone into that mix called political economy. It is not to be expected that everyone nudged by me should forever share my views, nor is such the case. Indeed, a few individuals who had their original interest aroused by my efforts have headed down the anarchistic road. Such people would eliminate government so that each person—in the absence of any societal agency—would be a law unto himself. These, however, are not the main object of my concern; rather, I am bothered by those who take the opposite tack, namely, the advocacy of more government to be rid of excessive government, that is, those who employ involuntary means and think thereby to widen voluntarism and individuality. What have I done—or left undone—to cause that!

Following a lecture of mine, the then President of the American Bar Association, nationally known for his conservatism, proclaimed, "The teaching of American history should be made compulsory." He thought he was lending support to my thesis.

Professor Benjamin Rogge has had experiences similar to mine:

> At the end of a FEE seminar, one of the participants in my discussion group stood up and said in absolute seriousness, "What we ought to have in every school and college in this country is a compulsory course in freedom."
>
> Let us not laugh too long at this well-meaning man until we have searched our own records to see how many times and in how many ways we have denied . . . the philosophy of freedom. . . .

Two persons, "turned on" at least partly by me, are proposing a bill in their state legislature making it compulsory to teach free enterprise economics in all public schools. As in other instances, it is an overwhelming eagerness to advance the observation and the practice of freedom principles that blinds them to the contradiction in their own proposals. Instead of "a step in the right direction," as they seem to think, their "remedies" would only add another compulsion to the compulsions they wish eliminated. They try to put out the fire by pouring fuel on it. Intentions fine, but the means are wrong!

Let us examine for a moment the idea of compelling school teachers to give courses in free enterprise economics. Imagine that you—a devotee of the freedom philosophy —are a public school teacher and that a bill has been passed compelling you to teach Marxism or other variants of socialism. You would be faced with the choice of either quitting or pretending. If the latter, the sham and insincerity would be evident even to dull students. Marxism could never be advanced with its adversaries as teachers.

Similarly with the free market, private ownership, limited government concepts. No one can teach this way of life who does not understand it or who is revolted by it. The vast majority of public school teachers have but a dim and distorted view of the market economy. Most of them could not teach free market economics if they tried; any attempts to force them to do so would only increase their resentment.

True, a course could be labeled "Free Market Economics." But who would select the textbooks? An agency of the state! What would be the nature of the text? It would deal in Keynesian terms with the total economy—macro economics—as do most of the economic textbooks now in use. Government officials could not be expected to choose otherwise. They operate outside the market.

And even if by some quirk of fate the state agency should select such books as Hazlitt's *Economics In One Lesson,* Ballve's *Essentials of Economics,* or Mises' *Human Action,* it would make little difference. The late Dr. Leo Wolman, long-time Professor of Economics at Columbia University, told me, "I spend all of my time in classes pointing out what is wrong with the reading material I am obliged to give my students." It is the teacher who teaches. He can use either Samuelson or Mises to lead the thinking his way.

Today, there are hundreds—not thousands—of teachers with considerable competence to explain free market economics. Their competence to do this came about not by compulsion but by volition: thinking for themselves and turning to such lights as came within their vision. This is the process and the only one that can hasten the teaching of freedom. A resort to compulsion can only kill the process.

Identifying the Role of Force

So, what accounts for this compulsive urge often evident in those with a newly aroused interest in freedom? Insofar as any of this is my responsibility, what have I been neglecting? Wherein lies my failure? A clue to the answer lies in the nature of the mischief: a resort to organized force as a means of reducing the employment of organized force in society. Obviously, I have failed to emphasize sufficiently that the nature of government is organized force and to show—in the light of its nature—the limited number of actions appropriate for government to take.

Anarchism—no societal agency at all—contends that there are no actions appropriate for government to take, that the advocacy of organized force to protect life and property cannot stop there but will continue to grow and undermine all life and property; admitting the propriety of any government sets the stage for all-out statism. Abandon the idea of government altogether, say the anarchists, or else expect it to become all-pervasive!

Anarchy—no government; each a law unto himself—must result in chaos. The strong will first subordinate the weak and then contend amoung themselves for territorial mastery. If socialism is planned chaos, then this is unplanned chaos! Neither socialism nor anarchism is tenable; and to settle on one or the other is to run away from the societal problem—an escape from reality!

Of course this problem is sticky. The best minds since the dawn of civilization have disputed over where to draw the line between the proper and the improper role for government. And never have the disagreements been more pronounced and numerous than in our time.

It is not that I have totally failed to draw the line, at least as I see it. Rather, I have done so only casually or as an aside: now and then in articles or on occasion in discussion sessions. It is becoming clear to me now that this matter of drawing the line in the employment of organized force is not something to be treated incidentally *but has to be made the very body of the case for freedom.* Short of this, we will continue to find our friends, if not ourselves, advocating compulsory courses in freedom and similar contradictions. So, this is one of the faults that looking in the mirror reveals to me.

My own now-and-then explanations have been built around an exposition of what organized force can and cannot do, such as set forth in the previous chapter. While this explanation satisfactorily serves me in my own efforts at drawing the line, it seems less than sufficient for many others. Perhaps they do not attach enough importance to this phase of the freedom rationale to think it through for themselves, in which case my attempted explanation does not really sink in. Or, maybe the distinction I perceive between inhibiting and creating is too vague or esoteric to be helpful to others in meeting their real-life problems. Doubtless, my own casualness tends to breed indifference among listeners and readers.

But more to the point, no one explanation, nor any person's unique way of phrasing it, will ever suffice. So, it's time to heed again the maxim, "If at first you don't succeed, try and try again."

Organized force—government—is precisely what the term implies. It is physical force or the threat thereof. It is now and forever just that and nothing else. A constabulary is a constabulary, be it "At ease" or in combat. A gun is always a gun, be it in the gun rack or in active use. The same can be said of a clenched fist or of a bouncer. The nature of organized force is a constant; never expect it to function other than according to its nature.

Organized force, however, may be employed in either of two radically different ways: *aggressively* or *defensively*. To illustrate: A policeman is a policeman. There he stands with gun in holster. With the force we have entrusted to him, he can enter your home, take your possessions, and dispose of them as he pleases. This is the *aggressive* employment of force. Or, he can stand guard and, hopefully, keep thieves and marauders from entering your home. This is the *defensive* employment of force. So, there we have precisely the same force employed in two distinctive and quite opposite ways!

I draw the line between no government and all-out government at that point where organized force departs from *defensive* employment and enters *aggressive* employment.[1] It is a line fairly easy to discern and accounts for my opposition to most of the current activities of our Federal,

---

[1] An equitable assessment to defray the costs of government limited to the defensive role is itself a defensive act and not—as sometimes charged —an aggressive one. For my explanation, see *Government: An Ideal Concept* (Irvington-on-Hudson, N.Y.: The Foundation for Economic Education, Inc., 1954), pp. 56-62.

state, and local governments. More than ever before in American history, governments at all levels employ *aggressive* force.

Therefore, that is where I would draw the line, my prescription for limited government. Note that government, thus limited, never initiates action, never aggresses. It engages exclusively in reactions to destructive actions, that is, the force is brought into play only as some members of society may initiate aggression against others. Otherwise, the force of government is passive or quiescent—in a standby position. Thus conceived, its role is to inhibit injustice, so that freedom and justice may prevail—no physical force or threat of force directed against the release of creative human energy!

The historical record is studded with examples of governments getting out of bounds and turning to all-out statism; and some conclude that the process is inevitable, that it must always be thus. Nonsense! Whether the line is properly drawn and scrupulously observed depends entirely on the importance we attach to this phase of the freedom rationale, on our attentiveness to it, and on our ability to understand and explain it. If such understanding becomes the consensus, limited government will prevail against all odds. "The condition upon which God hath given liberty to man is eternal vigilance." It is not in man's power to exact a better bargain; the price is vigilance, now and forever.

If your mirror reveals shortcomings like those I see in mine, then why not embark on some exploration and phrasing of your own? Who knows! Perhaps yours will catch on.

9 • TO AVARICE NO SANCTION

Avarice is wider than injustice, and all fallen nations lost liberty through avarice which engendered injustice.

—Austin O'Malley

● No POINT in the field of political economy merits more thought and analysis than where to draw the line distinguishing the functions proper to government from the role assumed by all-out government—socialism. A good society is but a dream unless this issue be reasonably resolved. Of all private decisions having to do with social problems, this heads the list.

I have in the two preceding chapters suggested two approaches, each satisfactory to me, as to where the line should be drawn. These ways, while not much refuted, find but scant acceptance by others. Perhaps there is no pat explanation, no magic key.

A comparable dilemma illustrates how near insoluble the problem is: Having observed countless individuals over the years who have switched from a socialist position to one favoring the freedom philosophy, I have, on each occasion, inquired as to the idea or experience that sparked the change. So far, no two have been identical; in a word, no magic key. What then is one to do? Are we helpless in getting others to see the merits of freedom? Is there anything in the way of exemplary living that will open their doors of perception? There appears to be a helpful procedure: See how many keys you can get on your own ring, that is, see how expansive you can make your own repertory. This carries no assurance, but it does increase the probability of success: there is always a greater probability that some one of a thousand keys will open that door than if only one key is picked at random.

Another Key to Limited Government

Similarly, with drawing the line on government; there is no magic key or explanation—apparently. What to do? Keep probing for more explanations; see how many keys one can find. So, here is another key I would offer: *Never admit a law to the statute books that makes an appeal to avarice.* Will this help to draw the line? Maybe yes and maybe no but, at least, it deserves reflection.

Again, is this fact: The essential nature of government is organized force. Expanded, this means laws backed by force. To know what government should and should not do, according to this key—where to draw the line—requires a judgment as to which laws appeal to avarice, and a decision to avoid such laws!

Next, observe a common characteristic of human beings, a trait relevant to the point in question: *"Man tends to satisfy his desires along the lines of least possible resistance.*"[1]

This, we must concede, is an overwhelming tendency. Rare, indeed, are the exceptions. Many wealthy citizens, for instance, applied for Medicare following enactment of the law. Nearly all religious, educational, and charitable organizations, although not compelled to partake in the "social security" program, rushed to the trough. Millions of our citizens accept unemployment payments in preference to working. Offer farmers more money for not farming than they can make by farming and they will not farm. Labor unions, given power to impose their will on others, tear the market to shreds. Businessmen generally hasten to forswear competition whenever protection is proffered; indeed, they will make machines to bring moon dirt back to earth if it be profitable to do such. These—appeals to avarice—are but a few among thousands of examples affirming the tendency to satisfy desires along the lines of least resistance.

Subsidies Attract "Clients"

For clarity, put this common tendency in another phrasing: Avarice breaks out, shows itself, grows and expands in proportion to the opportunities for a "free lunch" or a handout. Why? Simply because these feeding stations provide the means by which man can satisfy his desires along the lines of least resistance, offer him a way of overcoming his uneasiness without effort. Conceding some exceptions,

---

[1] Albert Jay Nock repeatedly referred to this as Epstean's Law.

men turn to these something-for-nothing sources as readily and as naturally as they turn away from higher and toward lower prices for goods and services. The bees go where the nectar is, avarice or no!

Exceptions to the rule have been noted. There are a few who will not stoop to the line of least resistance—persons whose moral guidelines will not let them live by bread alone. In the final analysis, a good society rests on a proliferation of this breed of men, however far removed we now are from that idealistic future. Meanwhile, it may be possible, by rationally conceiving where the line should be drawn, to effect a change for the better. But this will be difficult enough. The percentage of the population accustomed to the feeding stations is so great and their voting power so attractive to politicians who accommodate this weakness that the combination seems unbeatable. Nevertheless, it is worth a try.

Men stand upright in the absence of things to stoop for. The course of least resistance does not necessarily lead one astray if there is nothing to stoop for. Avarice is only a dormant trait in the absence of something to be avaricious about.

Feeding stations, contrived by laws that appeal to avarice, are composed exclusively of the fruits of people's labor—everyone of them. When these abound, as now, men *contend* with each other for our *property. They take!* Why? This is the line of least resistance. Remove these stations. Immediately men will *compete* with each other for our *favor. They trade!* Why? Because this is the remaining line of least resistance.

From stooping to upright men! From contenders to com-

petitors! From takers to traders! From plunderers to bene-
factors! No more goodness or perfection in man than before, but only the removal from his presence of the tempta-
tions to avarice!

How are we to judge whether or not a law has an appeal
to avarice, so that we may keep it off the statute books? I
believe there is a simple rule: *Never give approval to a law
that "helps" anyone!*

No Special Privileges

It is definitely not the function of government to take
positive action in aiding or sustaining or lending assistance
to any person or group or segment of society. Such "help"
can only be given to one person or group at the expense of
others. The only principled role of society's agency is negative; government should restrain anyone from doing injury
to others. The law's job is to codify the taboos or the thou-
shalt-nots and enforce them; that is, it should invoke a
common justice and keep the peace.

Any time and in every instance in which government departs from this negative or purely defensive role, avarice
is released in the citizenry. Government can do all of us a
service by warding off intruders; but when government pre-
tends to "help" us, government itself thereby becomes the
colossal intruder.

I am quite aware that to most people this way of drawing
the line seems cold, heartless, and without pity. But pity,
unless spiced with common sense, is what's heartless. Providing people with governmental feeding stations not only
kindles the vice of avarice but it renders them helpless. The

process results in an atrophy of the faculties from which recovery is next to impossible. *Helping people to become helpless is no act of kindness.* Nor is self-pity in order, that is, feeling sorry for ourselves as taxpayers. Such sympathy as is within us should be extended to the recipients of this largess, for they have stooped and may not be able to straighten up again.

No doubt a world in which matter never got out of place and became dirt, in which iron had no flaws and wood no cracks, in which gardens had no weeds, and food grew already cooked, in which clothes never wore out and washing was as easy as the soapmakers' advertisements describe it, in which rules had no exceptions and things never went wrong, would be a much easier place to live in. But for purposes of training and development it would be worth nothing at all.

It is the resistance that puts us on our mettle: it is the conquest of the reluctant stuff that educates the worker. I wish you enough difficulties to keep you well and make you strong and skillful![2]

This then is my third way to draw the line: To avarice no sanction!

---

[2]Henry Van Dyke.

10 • THE ROLE OF RULES

The first and most necessary topic in philosophy is the practical application of principles.
—Epictetus

● IT IS AN ACCEPTED NOTION in some circles that there are no norms or guidelines for human action. We are, it is said, creatures of impulse, responding to whatever notions pop into mind. "Radical relativism," as it is called, invites re-examination of the way of life founded on rules and principles. There seems to be considerable confusion about the nature and purpose of rules.

An aphorism may help put the point in focus: "Rules are meant for those expected to obey; principles for those expected to think." This seems to suggest that rules are made by dictators to be obeyed by slaves and that principles are the findings of philosophers to be savored and pondered by thinkers. But such a conclusion is far too shallow.

The principle of a thing is a verbal formulation of its nature and its workings; a rule is a homely guide to action deduced from the principle.

There are good rules and bad rules precisely as there are true and false principles. A good rule: "Do not unto others that which you would not have them do unto you." A bad rule: "The king can do no wrong." Now to principles: "The earth revolves on its axis and around the sun" (Copernicus) is a principle upon which man may rely. An earlier theory, "The sun revolves around the earth" (Ptolemy) has now been rejected as a true principle because it has been proved to be inadequate. Rules derived from the principles of Copernicus may be followed with assurance and may not safely be ignored.

Ptolemy's theory afforded no basis for the law of gravitation. Rules deduced from such a theory would prove disastrous. Example: a medical officer attached to the Air Force in the Far East during WW II told me of a B-29 Captain whose mission was to transport some fifty Chinese coolies to a labor assignment. Half way to his destination and at 18,000 feet, he visited the cabin to check on his charges. Some missing! How come? Later, from a peekhole position, he observed that they had opened a hatchway. Two of them made a saddle of their hands on which one of their buddies would sit, all three laughing as they tossed him out! These people knew nothing of the law of gravitation and, of course, could not observe the results. To them, it was only to fly through the air like a bird!

No one knows precisely how to explain gravitation, yet many of us know that it works and we frame countless rules accordingly: for instance, we do not jump off the Empire State Building. To disregard these rules is to court disaster.

Principles, discovered by philosophers and scientists, abound by the thousands. Yet, most of us are unaware of many of these principles. Even the vast majority of philosophers and scientists have not the slightest idea about each other's formulations. Who among them, for instance, knows of the subjective and marginal utility theory of value or the principle of freedom in transactions? Perhaps one, now and then—a rarity! Had we no way of abiding by principles except as we understand them, man would perish from the earth.

Specialists Gone Astray

One of the world's great astronomers comes to mind. In his field he is tops. And because he sees more through his little peekhole than others with similar peekholes, he ventures with self-assurance into politico-economic matters about which he knows next to nothing. Over and over again we witness geniuses in their particular specializations assuming a knowledge of areas in which they have no competence. Follow this astronomer in astronomy and become enlightened; follow him in political economy and become enslaved. Specialization, when coupled with man's arrogance, leads toward such danger.

What then is our saving grace? Rules! Do not touch a red hot stove or a live wire; do not jump out of a plane without a parachute; do not cheat, lie, steal, kill; do not feather your own nest at the expense of others. I do not have to know that "The volume of a gas varies inversely as the pressure" to avoid a bomb exploding in my face. I only need to know the rule, "Don't play with bombs."

Let us now turn to the idea that "Rules are meant for those expected to obey." True, perhaps, but what is the nature of these rules? There are two divisions—poles apart and each requiring its distinct kind of obedience. Rules in the first category are psychological in nature and obedience consists in practicing self-discipline; those in the second are sociological in nature and obedience consists in submitting to external authority.

Take the Golden Rule, which is a maxim in the first category. This is the oldest ethical proposition of distinctly universal character. If one is intelligent enough to see the wisdom of this rule and if he has the strength of character to heed it, he obeys. Otherwise, not! Each individual makes his own decision to obey or not, and there is no external authority on earth, no government that has the slightest power to exact obedience to such a rule. Intelligence and strength of character are never the products of external compulsion but are exclusively voluntary and of one's own making. Is this not self-evident?

The Commandment, "Thou shalt not covet," is but another of countless ethical and moral rules—a rule that is obeyed or not as the individual chooses. A gun at my head could not keep me from coveting another's achievements or possessions. These are secrets of the soul, intellect, and conscience. Such secrets are not necessarily revealed to others or understood by them. No matter how stupid or wrong my secret longings, they are not subject to correction by external compulsion. In these matters each decides on the rules to be accepted or rejected and he prospers or fails in life's purpose according to how intelligently he identifies the rules and obeys them.

Once we recognize our shortcomings in understanding and obeying these ethical and moral rules and guidelines

—an area in which the individual is in complete command and without interference—we must conclude that man by nature is imperfect. Regardless of how well we know these rules and how obediently we observe them, we will, to some extent, offend the rights of others. Perfect harmony in society is not possible, even among the moral and spiritual elite. And pronounced indeed is the disharmony caused by those who have no scruples—no rules of their own!

Rules Against Antisocial Behavior

This poses the necessity for rules of the second kind, those that are sociological in nature. These are meant to take effect if and when moral laws are ignored or violated; they are designed to cope with the antisocial as distinguished from the peaceful actions of citizens, that is, with those actions which cause injury to others. Injury, as the term is applied in this context, must be carefully defined by rules, which if properly drawn and obeyed, would assure a fair field and no favor. In this category of rules, we are expected to obey *not necessarily* what our conscience suggests but, rather, what an external authority dictates. As distinguished from moral law, this is civil law; it punishes those who trespass against their fellows, but it presupposes that there are men who behave ethically a good part of the time.

It is utter folly to believe that there can be a good society without the rule of law—civil law, that is. Yet, this category of rules is loaded with the possibility for evil as well as good results. Civil law can, and often does, lead to total statism—enslavement—or it can, but rarely does, lead to securing individual liberty. Nonetheless, the free society is out of the question in the absence of civil law; to have even the remotest chance of the good society requires that we assume the risk that civil law might go askew. To achieve the best, we must face and overcome grave dangers. There is no alternative!

Wherein lies our hope? Is there, indeed, a certain narrow course which, if scrupulously followed, would secure liberty to all alike and which would, at the same time, steer away from lawless anarchy on the one side and all-out statism on the other? If so, what is it?

There is definitely and explicitly such a course and it can be ours if we are not blind to it. The price tag, however, is the ability to see and, having seen, to stay on course.

Endowed by the Creator

This high road has as its foundation what many early Americans believed—and I devoutly believe—to be a wholly reasonable presupposition, namely, that men's rights to life, livelihood, and liberty are endowed by the Creator. These rights are part of our very being, and our being, although it is compounded of elements deriving from our society and other ingredients that link us with nature, is rooted in a reality which transcends both nature and society. Each man participates in an order which confers upon him certain prerogatives which other men should not impair.

This proposition gains confirmation as we reflect on the absurdity of its only possible alternative, namely, that men's rights to life, livelihood, and liberty are endowed by a human collective which, in this context, is government. Of what is government composed? Persons no more graced with virtues, talents, and omniscience than you or I! For any human being to believe that our rights to life, livelihood, and liberty are or could be derived from him is nothing less than egomania.

This inherent rights principle, affirmed in the Declaration of Independence, has fallen by the wayside so far as comprehension and acceptance are concerned. Giving the reasons, beyond a growing egomania, is no less difficult than trying to explain the decline in religion, that is, the rejection of an Infinite Power or Intelligence over and beyond our little, finite minds.

There is, however, an easily misunderstood companion idea in the Declaration that may have led many people astray: ". . . that all men are created equal." This has been seized upon by the Declaration's detractors to "prove" how nonsensical its writers were in whatever they declared, including the Creator concept. Of course men are not equal in a single personal attribute. This is so obvious that the authors of the Declaration took no pains to say so. They were not writing to fools. What they had in mind was the profound idea that *all men are equal before the civil law as they are before God.* This relegates civil law to its proper place. Without this concept of equality before the law, justice is out of the question and civil law is out to get you and me. As Professor Benjamin Rogge puts it, "The blindfolded Goddess of Justice is encouraged to peek: 'Tell me who you are and I shall tell you what your rights are.' "

Finally, these two kinds of rules work one on the other —they are interacting. It is ridiculous to believe that any set of civil laws can be devised to bring about the good society among a people having no moral and ethical scruples. On the other hand, whenever a first-rate citizenry carelessly permits the civil law to go beyond its principled scope of maintaining the peace of the community, it will deprive them of their liberty and self-responsibility. In this event, they will degenerate into law breakers, black marketeers, connivers.

Those who aspire to a good society have no manner of realizing their goal except as they (1) understand and obey the basic principles or rules of morality and ethics, and (2) establish and limit the scope of civil law so as to insure liberty and justice for all.

Thus, the first-rate citizen has a dual role to perform as related to the role of rules.

11 • HARMONIZING TO EACH HIS OWN

Weep not that the world changes—did it keep a stable, changeless state, 'twere cause indeed to weep.

—Bryant

• MAN COULD NOT LIVE, let alone improve his lot, were all static as a rock. Change releases the hidden strength of men. Out of change comes variation and in this diversity are unique potentialities realized. Creative dissimilarities emerge and account for our moral, spiritual, intellectual, and material wealth. Change is of the very essence of life, and freedom to change is both an economic and a biologic necessity.

The enormity and persistence of change and variation is recognized and welcomed by some, though most persons tend to dislike it. "Change, indeed, is painful, yet ever needed," said Carlyle; inevitable and necessary but, nonetheless, much resented. This feature of human nature poses a major politico-economic problem and substantially ac-

counts for the continuing debate over freedom versus coercive collectivism.

The main reason for resenting change, I suspect, origi-
nates in a misunderstanding of how security is best ob-
tained. Individuals, with rare exceptions, are interested
first and foremost in securing life and livelihood. Security
is indeed an objective but, contrary to general belief, it is
never more than a dividend of natural change and variation
—each pursuing his own uniqueness. There is no security to
be found in bringing change and variation to a halt; nothing is so at odds with security as freezing or solidifying
the status quo. Seek first security and there will be neither
security nor change. Seek first the dynamic, improving
life and such security as is possible is thrown in as a rewarding outcome.[1]

To intelligently approach the politico-economic problem
here posed requires, first of all, that we fully grasp just
how fantastic our variations really are, else we will not
know what the problem is or the meaning of "to each his
own." Gloss over our variations, think of them as less than
they are, and we will behave as unwitting, mindless persons.

Let us face a few facts. We resemble each other in out-

---

[1]Change, as I am extolling it, refers only to those forms induced in the
exercise of free choice. The enormous technological changes resulting
from present coercive practices—moon ventures, for example—are, in my
view, disruptive, unbalancing, and uneconomic. They lead creativity
toward "national goals" or political designs and away from subjective
value judgments; they make for insecurity. The trouble is, we see the
mooncraft and generally adjudge it wonderful. What we fail to see are
the inevitable and disastrous consequences of—reactions to—the coercion
which brought this fantastic gadget into being.

ward appearance only: beings with two eyes, one nose, ten fingers, two arms, standing upright on two legs, and somewhat alike in other superficial ways. Even in these ways the variation is fantastic, "identical twins" being far from identical.[2]

Human beings are distinguished from the animal world by the possession of such traits as the ability to reason, to evaluate different causes of action, to make rational choices, to will their own behaviors, and even to transcend themselves. So varied are these potentialities and their mode of realization that resemblances diminish sharply; we go every which way, in as many directions as each person takes in a lifetime multiplied by all the human beings who ever lived. Chaos, seemingly!

Infinite Variation

The human scene holds no such thing as a changeless, single performance with which to compare, to identify, to judge our works. At the human level there are as many kinds and qualities of performances as there are viewpoints. Thus, the variety of performances equals all the people who have ever lived times all the changing viewpoints each person ever experiences. Trillions times trillions!

This assertion itself is a personal viewpoint or evaluation and argues that the eye of the beholder is determinative. "Were the eye not attuned to the Sun, the Sun could

---

[2]See various works by Roger Williams, especially *You Are Extraordinary* (New York: Random House, 1967).

never be seen by it," wrote Goethe. Viewpoints, by and large, are based on major and easily observed distinctions. For instance, I glance at a smiling face and a moment later at the same face when angry. The distinction evokes two evaluations, varying viewpoints easily come by. But widen the aperture to increase sensitivity to infinitesimal changes, and even assuming no change in outward demeanor: the face is known to be older; the lighting is different; I have aged; and my vision has changed. The world of anyone sensitive to a wide range of variations is a far larger world than exists for those who are not so graced, that is, his viewpoints and evaluations are greatly multiplied.

Or reflect on what the world means to a farmer and to an astronomer. A particular farmer may be satisfied with treading the surface of our planet and scratching it with a plow; his world is a road, some furrows, and a field of grain. The astronomer's world, on the other hand, requires that he determine exactly the place that it occupies at each instant within sidereal space; from the standpoint of exactness he is forced to convert our globe into a mathematical abstraction, into a case of universal gravitation. We might say that the farmer and the astronomer "are worlds apart."[3]

In order to picture the enormity of variation, consider the varying evaluations or viewpoints of each farmer times all the farmers there are and then of all the astronomers since Copernicus and Galileo times all their changing viewpoints during these past four centuries. And last, contem-

---

[3]The idea and some of the phrasing in this paragraph are from an essay, "Adán en el Paraiso" (Adam in Paradise) 1910 by José Ortega y Gasset.

plate all the performances there have been beyond the farmer and the astronomer and all the performances that lie between these two and all the varying evaluations thereof!

We can now see that it is the point of view that creates the variation panorama: an infinitude of performances in a constant flux. No person can do more than to become aware of this complexity; few even do this. To encompass this multiplicity, to bring it within anyone's comprehension, is out of the question. Initially, such awareness cannot help but breed confusion. How can harmony ever be brought out of this social maelstrom!

The Individual in Society

Confusion, however, does not end here. It starts anew with countless attempts at harmonizing our variations. The confusion appears to stem from a fact seldom recognized in clarity: man is at once a social and an individualistic being. Confronting each of us are the we and the I or, one might say, association and isolation. Not only is there myself to cope with: to grow, emerge, evolve, to become what I am not yet; equally challenging, I must find out how to live in harmony with my fellowmen. My life and welfare depend not only on what I make of me but also on how I associate myself with others upon whom I am also rigorously dependent, a dependence from which there is no escape. Except in association, I perish! No need to labor this point.

Thus, two extremely intricate problems are posed. The first is psychological in nature: freeing self from superstitions, imperfections, ignorance, fears. We know far less about this than is generally acknowledged. The second is sociological, that is, freeing men from the restraints and impositions which we in our ignorance are inclined to inflict on each other. Unless the latter is reasonably resolved, the former cannot flourish at its best. Yet, a resolution of the latter is impossible without a flourishing of the former. Boxed in by a paradox! Or are we?

There are, broadly, two opposed theories as to how the sociological maelstrom should be resolved. The first—authoritarian—is steeped in tradition, as aged as humanity, and presently gaining ground all over the world. It is the old, old master-slave arrangement that has always stifled human progress and diverted man's efforts to fighting, either to force his will on others or to combat the tyrant's army. The second—freedom—is brand new as history goes, all too seldom understood or accepted.

Authoritarian Confusion

Perhaps no statement more openly and honestly reveals the authoritarian confusion than this:

> Only a moron would believe that the millions of private economic decisions being made independently of each other will somehow harmonize in the end and bring us out where we want to be.[4]

Where we want to be! Here is the authoritarian position set forth in crystal clarity: an *I* pretending to be a *we*. It is safe to assume that no earthly person wants to be what

---

[4] The late Walter Reuther. See *The New York Times*, June 30, 1962.

the author wanted to be at the moment of this phrasing. One knows, without looking at the record, that this author experienced a constant shifting in what he wanted to be during every day of his life. The same can be said of Napoleon or any of our numerous political authoritarians, precisely as can be said of you or me. No living person ever stays put; as to our aspirations, all of us are in flight, on the wing, in orbit. We need do no more than look about us to confirm this fact.

The point is that no person who ever lived—not even Socrates—has observed more than an infinitesimal fraction of the total universe. Each gazes through a tiny peekhole into infinity, glimpsing hardly any of it. Did Hitler see the farmer's furrow or what Galileo saw or what I see as I write or you see as you read these scribblings? Of course not! The authoritarian vision is limited and blurred at best.

What then must be the outcome of the authoritarian's solution to social problems, assuming that his will is invoked? Simple: all of us compelled to abide by what he sees through his unique and tiny peekhole which, of course, is next to nothing. All of us, if his will prevails, restricted by his oblique view of reality.

Most appraisals of authoritarianism are not as harsh as mine because no one has ever witnessed the horrible principle in more than partial practice. We observe people living, a few rather prosperously, in Russia, China, Uruguay and falsely credit such of the good life as there is to the authoritarianism. To the contrary, it is in spite of! All that is good—*no exception*— springs from creative human energy obeying its nature, that is, freely flowing when not squelched. Like lightning, it zigs and zags along the line of least resistance, finding its way through or around the commands and strictures of he-who-knows-next-to-no-thing. A harsh appraisal of the authoritarian? No; that rating applies to all of us!

How Freedom Works Its Wonders

A supervisor of schools, attending one of our workshops recently, made this observation concerning freedom as a solution to social problems:

> I came to your Summer Seminar with a hazy and limited knowledge of the principles of economics and the free market. You have helped me to see the simplicity and self-evidence of these basic concepts of freedom. *What most amazes me now is that anyone can fail to understand and put these ideas into practice.*

Yes, the simplicity of freedom in action as it copes with infinite human variation and works its wonders! Amazing indeed that so many are unaware of these principles and thus have no faith in them. Parenthetically, any proposed solution to the social and individualistic aspects of humanity that is not simple has nothing to commend it. This is another way of saying that we should stick to what we know best—our own knitting—which, as already suggested, is not very much.

Let me now return to the assertion, "Only a moron would believe that the millions of private economic decisions being made independently of each other will somehow harmonize in the end and bring us out where we want to be." I read this statement ten years ago and not until now did I realize that the author was substantially correct.

Why? Only a person deficient in reasoning powers—not necessarily a moron—could possibly believe that any scheme can "bring us out where we want to be." This is an *I* posing as *we*—absurd! The flowering society, the only kind that merits our interest, is one that will not stand in the way of bringing you out where *you* want to be, while permitting the same opportunities for everyone else. And this is definitely a prospect when millions—yes, trillions—of decisions are made independently of each other, that is, a situation in which freedom of choice prevails.

It is an observed fact that variation obtains throughout the natural order; it is a distinguishing feature of the universal scheme of things ranging from atoms and their components to galaxies which are but tiny parts of who knows what. No two things are identical—no two snowflakes or stars or sunsets or tidal waves. Everything at all times and in all places and in all circumstances is in motion. But note that instead of chaos there is order and stability—an incomprehensible harmony—and because of a mysterious principle at work:

> All the phenomena of astronomy, which had baffled the acutest minds since the dawn of history, the movement of the heavens, of the sun and the moon, the very complex movement of the planets, suddenly tumble together and become intelligible in terms of the one staggering assumption, this mysterious "attractive force."[5]

These variations we observe in nature, by reason of this "mysterious attractive force," gravitate into a harmony;

---

[5]See *Science is a Sacred Cow* by Anthony Standen (New York: E. P. Dutton and Company, Inc., 1950), pp. 63-64.

that is, there is an inexplicable magnetism constantly, everlastingly exerting itself. And precisely this same force operates in exactly the same manner on the fantastically varied out-croppings of the human cortex: viewpoints, evaluations, inventions, insights, intuitive flashes, think-of-thats.

Harmonious Creative Energy

Who understands creative human energy? Who can define it? No one! It is as mysterious and indefinable as electrical energy. Indeed, the two behave in much the same manner: they naturally flow along the lines of least resistance. The point is, we live without understanding Creation or life; electricity and gravitation serve even though we haven't the slightest idea as to what they are; the same is true of creative human energy—provided we leave it free to flow.

What at first blush appears as utter chaos—a veritable hurricane of flighty performances—turns out to be precisely the opposite: a harmonic whole in the absence of *I's* trying to play *we*. You to your knitting, me to mine, each pursuing his unique potential, be it farming or astronomy or whatever. For only in this manner am I able to draw on your and everyone else's unique realizations, others possessing countless ideas, enlightenments, goods, services hardly any one of which is within my own potential. When freedom prevails, we can think of our situation as a vast human grid, supplies responding to demands in a perpetual willing exchange. *A harmonizing of to each his own!*

We cannot know how freedom, any more than Creation,

works its wonders. Nor do we need to know the how of it. We need only know (1) that freedom does work wonders—the evidence is commonplace and all about us—and (2) that freedom exists in the absence of man-concocted restraints against the release of creative energy. And observe how simple—and realistic—this is: it does not presuppose a single know-it-all!

12 • HOW EVERYONE CAN GAIN

*I volunteer to exchange mine for thine
because I prefer thine to mine. You freely
consent to the exchange when you prefer
mine to thine. Each of us gains, in his own
eyes—the only relevant test in these matters.*

● MANY A PERSON afflicted with nearsighted-
ness has been enabled, by eye exercises, to throw away his
spectacles and see as well as ever. In the economic realm,
nearsightedness seems to be a common condition. I contend that a respectable vision can be gained by a few mental exercises. To employ Bastiat's phrasing, let us examine
"that which is seen and that which is not seen," specifical-
ly as related to economic gain and loss. For unless our vision is clear in this respect, we will mistake losses for
gains and vice versa.

There is a prevailing notion that anybody's gain must be
at someone else's expense, that the riches of one derive
from pauperizing the many, that winners presuppose losers.
It is important to see why this notion persists and why it is
utterly false.

Were we to collapse the span of mankind into one year, the notion that one's gain is another's loss had some validity until about 7 hours ago. Prior to the eighteenth century, most of man's exchanges were of the winner-take-all type.

Recall that in ancient times robbery was the first labor-saving device. Hordes from one nation raided a neighboring nation, taking home the loot. The raiders thought they saw gain in the process; the raided knew they lost.

Later, feudalism prevailed; that is, there was very little private ownership as we understand it. Estates and most possessions were political conferments: dukedoms, earldoms, lord of the manor type of economic arrangements. These holdings of the few pauperized the many. Born a shoemaker, stay a shoemaker! All gain (?) for the few and all loss for the many.

Then, for a time before the industrial revolution, mercantilism became the style. "There are many points of resemblance between the mercantile system and state socialism . . . the policy of regulating industry and commerce with a view to national interests as distinct from those of the consumer."[1] Featured by price-fixing and special privilege, it was a closed system, favoring (?) the few at the expense of the many.

The Urge to Gamble

The above is only to emphasize the traditional experiences which work so powerfully against acceptance of re-

---

[1]See "Mercantile System," *Palgreaves Dictionary of Political Economy* (London: Macmillan and Co., 1926), Vol. II, p. 726.

cent enlightenments. Can man, in the latest 1/5,000th of his life on earth, free himself from the irrational mold into which he has so long been cast? Can man be expected so instantaneously to come to grips with this gain-loss fallacy?

It is too much to expect that any substantial number of people can succeed in this rational feat. For in addition to overcoming the ingrained notions of mankind's past, there are current experiences observed by everyone where one's loss is, in fact, another's gain. This is true in gambling, for instance: the turn of a card, the cast of a die, the flip of a coin. It is easy enough to make wrong deductions from these observations. We have to bear in mind that such gambling is not exchange in the economic or market sense. Trade is not involved; this is not something for something but, rather, something for nothing. Nonetheless, it is the source of bad instruction and leads many people to the false conclusion that, in every kind of exchange, one person's gain is necessarily someone else's loss.

When this notion prevails, as now, people adopt the attitude, "We might as well get ours while the getting is good." They are heedless of what their getting costs others, for is it not ordained that each gain must be attended by a loss? Thus, get ours, and "let the devil take the hindmost." All of this is precisely at the intellectual level of looting neighbors, feudalism, mercantilism, gambling. Contrary to what these people believe, no one gains; all are losers.

To illustrate: The Gateway Arch in St. Louis is not "The gateway to the West" itself; no one passes through that arch. Rather, it is but a symbol of the idea. So, let us use this symbol to symbolize the "get ours" syndrome. It is as good as any other of countless thousands.

Most of the local citizens—there are exceptions—think favorably of this multi-million dollar stainless steel structure. There it stands in all its awesome beauty for everyone to see—all gain and no loss they naively believe. The truth? This modern pyramid is all loss to everyone and no gain to anyone!

The Arch is heavily financed by Federal funds; you and I and millions of other out-of-town taxpayers were *coerced* to put into it a part of our lives. With no interest in this costly decorative symbol, ours is loss pure and simple. This is a fact beyond question.

A Vicious Circle

But what about the local citizens who think that the Gateway Arch is a gain—at least to them? Is theirs actually a loss and not a gain? Yes, false impressions to the contrary notwithstanding. Let me explain.

By requesting and accepting Federal funds they become a party to the "get ours" parade. When they endorse confiscation from millions of out-of-towners to build their local pet project, they thereby endorse similar enslavement of themselves to help build countless other pet projects all over the nation. *Intake: one arch; outgo: more than the arch cost!* All loss; no gain! What do the people of the United States have to show for all of these coercive actions? Thousands upon thousands of pet projects, each an economic monstrosity which would never have been built within the frame of the market; any project that is economically feasible is accomplished without coercion.

For one more example of nearsightedness, of how coercion results in all loss and no gain, have a look at above-market wage rates as effected by present-day labor union practices. No question about it, employers lose. And so do consumers, all citizens being consumers. It takes no economist to see this.

But what about labor union members, the ones who receive these excessive wages? Do they, also, lose? Yes, false impressions to the contrary! This, too, needs explanation.

When Trade Is Hampered

That we are an interdependent society is self-evident. I cannot live by the little I do or know how to do, nor can anyone else. Our survival now hinges on specialization and the free, uninhibited exchanges of our numerous specializations. We are wired up far more intricately than any computer—in an enormous human circuit, so to speak. A breakdown here or there—cut off electricity, telephones, planes, trains, trucks, garbage disposal, hospital service, mail delivery, or whatever—and the whole economy is fractured. Indeed, we have progressed so far in specialization, become so interdependent, that I cannot do any injury to you without that injury bouncing back and harming me. And this goes for labor union members, also. Their coercive practices tear the whole economy to shreds, the economy on which they are totally dependent, even as you and I. True, their nearsightedness lets them see what looks like a momentary advantage but leaves them blind to their lifetime interests. Any momentary result, regardless of appearance, should it contribute to long-range loss, must be counted as a loss and never a gain.

Each coercive act must, by its very nature, result in a loss not only to those acted upon but to the actors.[2] The thief loses something far more valuable than the loot he takes. The act "has cost him his peace, and the best of his manly virtues." In activities embraced by coercion—nationalized businesses, for example—certain gains may be observed; these are, more often than not, falsely attributed to the coercion. Such gains are due exclusively to a leakage of free, creative, human energy, an energy that has escaped the coercive embrace.

The process whereby everyone can gain, with no loss to anyone, is such a common occurrence—as breathing—that hardly anyone heeds or understands it, virtually a secret. Yet, simple as seven times seven and, if anything, easier to explain!

No Coercion Whatsoever

No man-concocted restraints against the release of creative energy, that is, no coercion, none whatsoever! That's all there is to it. In the absence of coercion, the free market exists. All exchanges are then to the *mutual* advantage of each trader, and cannot help but be. When I swap my $50 for your watch, I value the watch more than the $50

---

[2]Coercion as here used is the aggressive as distinguished from the defensive employment of physical force—or the threat thereof. Coercion is initiated force.

and you value the $50 more than the watch, else we would not exchange. Value in this equation is now and forever a subjective judgment. There is no other way to determine the value of a good or service than what you or I voluntarily give up to get it.[3]

Bastiat, when explaining the provisioning of Paris, had this to say about the miracle of the market:

How does each succeeding day manage to bring to this gigantic market just what is necessary—neither too much nor too little? What, then, is the resourceful and secret power that governs the amazing regularity of such complicated movements, a regularity in which everyone has such implicit faith, although his prosperity and his very life depend upon it? That power is an *absolute principle,* the principle of free exchange.[4]

And I shall now suggest two other absolutes: (1) In coerced exchanges everyone loses; no one gains and (2) in free market exchanges everyone gains; no one loses.

Do not these few observations bring an end to the nearsightedness that turns men toward coercion rather than voluntary exchange? If so, away with the spectacles! Let us practice freedom.

---

[3]For an explanation of this point, see "The Dilemma of Value" in my *Talking to Myself* (Irvington-on-Hudson, N.Y.: The Foundation for Economic Education, Inc., 1970), pp. 81-88.

[4]See *Economic Sophisms* by Frederic Bastiat (Irvington-on-Hudson, N.Y.: The Foundation for Economic Education, Inc., 1968), pp. 97-98.

13 • ECONOMICS: A BRANCH OF MORAL PHILOSOPHY

. . . science is inseparably attached to value judgments, especially the moral sciences, to which the social sciences . . . belong, and every attempt to eliminate these would end only in absurdity.

—Röpke

● THE AUTHOR OF *The Wealth of Nations* (1776) is frequently classed as an eighteenth century economist. But Adam Smith was primarily a Professor of Moral Philosophy, the discipline which I believe is the appropriate one for the study of human action and such subdivisions of it as may be involved in political economy.

Moral philosophy is the study of right and wrong, good and evil, better and worse. These polarities cannot be translated into quantitative and measurable terms and, for that reason, moral philosophy is sometimes discredited as lacking scientific objectivity. And it is not, in fact, a science in the sense that mathematics, chemistry, and physics are sciences. The effort of many economists to make the study of political economy a natural science draws the subject out of its broader discipline of moral philosophy, which leads in turn to social mischief.

Carl Snyder, long-time statistician of the Federal Reserve Board, exemplifies an economic "scientist." He wrote an impressive book, *Capitalism The Creator*, now out of print.[1]

I agree with this author that Capitalism is, indeed, a creator, providing untold wealth and material benefits to countless millions of people. But, in spite of all the learned views to the contrary, I believe that Capitalism, in its significant sense, is more than Snyder and many other statisticians and economists make it out to be—far more. If so, then to teach that Capitalism is fully explained in mathematical terms is to settle for something less than it really is. This leaves unexplained and vulnerable the real case for Capitalism.

Snyder equates Capitalism with "Capital Savings." He explains what he means in his Preface:

The thesis here presented is simple, and unequivocal; in its general outline, not new. What is new, I would fain believe, is the proof; clear, statistical, and factual evidence. That thesis is that there is one way, and only one way, that any people, in all history, have ever risen from barbarism and poverty to affluence and culture; and that is by that concentrated and highly organized system of production and exchange which we call Capitalistic: one way, and one alone. Further, that it is solely by the accumulation (and concentration) of this Cap-

---

[1]*Capitalism The Creator* by Carl Snyder (New York: The Macmillan Company, 1940), 473 pp.

ital, and directly proportional to the amount of this accumulation, that the modern industrial nations have
arisen; perhaps the sole way throughout the whole of
eight or ten thousand years of economic history.

No argument—none whatsoever—as to the accomplish-
ments of Capitalism, or that it has to do with "Capital Savings." But what is Capital?

The Spiritual Origin of Capital

The first answer that comes to mind is that Capital
means the tools of production: brick and mortar in the form
of plants, electric and water and other kinds of power,
machines of all kinds including computers and other
automated things, ships at sea and trains and trucks and
planes—you name it! These things are indeed Capital, but
is Capital in the sense of material wealth sufficient to tell
the whole story of Capitalism and its creative accomplish-
ments or potentialities?

Merely bear in mind that all of this fantastic gadgetry
on which rests a high standard of living has its origin in
ideas, inventions, discoveries, insights, intuition, think-of-
thats, and such other unmeasurable qualities as the will to
improve, the entrepreneurial spirit, intelligent self-interest,
honesty, respect for the rights of others, and the like. These
are spiritual as distinguished from material or physical assets, and always the former precedes and is responsible
for the latter. This is Capital in its fundamental, originating sense; this accumulated wisdom of the ages—an over-
all luminosity—is the basic aspect of "Capital Savings."

It is possible to become aware of this spiritual Capital,

but not to measure, let alone to fully understand it—so enormous is its accumulation over the ages. Awareness? Sit in a jet plane and ask what part you had in its making. Very little, if any, even though you might be on the production line at Boeing. At most, you pressed a button that turned on forces about which you know next to nothing. Why, no man even knows how to make the pencil you used to sign a requisition. These "Capital Savings" put at your disposal an energy perhaps several hundred times your own. This accumulated energy—the workings of human minds over the ages—is Capital!

With this concept of Capital in mind, reflect on how unrealistic are the ambitions of the "scientific" economists. Carl Snyder phrases their intentions well in the concluding paragraph of his Preface:

> It was inevitable, perhaps, that anything like a "social science" should be the last to develop. Its bases are so largely *statistical* that it was only with the development of an enormous body of new knowledge that anything resembling a firmly grounded and *truly scientific system* could be established. It is coming; already the most fundamental elements of this knowledge are now available, as the pages to follow will endeavor to set forth. (Italics added)

Snyder is, indeed, statistical. He displays 44 charts. Nearly all of these show the ups and downs—mostly ups— of physical assets in dollar terms. This, in his view, is a "truly scientific system." But how scientific can a measurement be if the units cannot be quantified and the measuring rod is as imprecise in value as is the dollar or any other monetary unit?

Not Subject to Scientific Measurement

And what is truly scientific about showing the growth in coal production, for instance, if there be a shift in demand favoring some other fuel? This would be only a pseudo measurement with no more scientific relevance than a century-old chart showing the dollar growth in buggy whip production.

Professor F. A. Hayek enlightens us:

> . . . all the "physical laws of production" which we meet, e.g., in economics, are not physical laws in the sense of the physical sciences but people's beliefs about what they can do. . . . That the objects of economic activity cannot be defined in objective terms but only with reference to a human purpose goes without saying. Neither a "commodity" or an "economic good," nor "foods" or "money," can be defined in physical terms but only in terms of views people hold about things.[2]

Economic growth for a nation cannot be mathematically or statistically measured. Efforts to do so are highly misleading. They lead people to believe that a mere increase in the measured output of goods and services is, in and of itself, economic growth. This fallacy has led to the forced savings programs of centrally administered economic systems—programs which decrease the range of voluntary choice among individuals. This is the heart of the failure of the socialistic policies of the underdeveloped nations of Asia, Africa, and Latin America. As Prof. P. T. Bauer has

---

[2]See *The Counter-Revolution of Science* by F. A. Hayek (New York: The Free Press of Glencoe, The Crowell-Collier Publishing Co., 1964), p. 31.

written so eloquently: "I regard the extension of the range of choice, that is, an increase in the range of effective alternatives open to people, as the principal objective and criterion of economic development; and I judge a measure principally by its probable effects on the range of alternatives open to individuals."[3]

Values Are Subjective, Personal Views

Indeed, even an individual's economic growth can no more be measured, exclusively, in terms of historical statistics than can his intellectual, moral, and spiritual growth. These ups and downs "cannot be defined in physical terms but only in terms of views people hold about things." These views—highly personal—are in constant flux; you may care nothing tomorrow for that which you highly prize today.

Once we grasp the point that the value of any good or service is whatever others will give in willing exchange, and that the judgments of all parties to all exchanges are constantly and forever changing, it should be plain that even physical assets—money, food, or whatever—do not lend themselves to measurements in the scientific sense.

And when we further reflect on the fundamental nature of "Capital Savings,"—that they emerge out of ideas, inventions, insights, and the like—the idea of scientific measurement becomes patently absurd.

In any event, it is this penchant to make a science of political economy, to reduce Capitalistic behavior to charts,

---

[3]P. T. Bauer, *Economic Analysis and Policy in Underdeveloped Countries* (Duke University Press and Cambridge University Press, 1957), p. 113.

statistics, theorems, arbitrary symbols, that leads to such nonsense as the Gross National Product (GNP), "national goals" and "social gains."[4] The more pronounced this trend, the less will the economics of Capitalism and the free society be understood—"a dismal science," for certain. Indeed, could the ambitions of the "scientific economists" be realized, dictatorship would be a viable political system. At the dictator's disposal would be all the formulae, all the answers; disregarding personal views and choices he would simply run his information through computers and thus meet production schedules.

Imperfect Man

When we grasp the point that no man who ever lived has been able to foresee his own future choices, let alone those of others, economic scientism, as it might be called, makes no sense.

How did we ever get off on this untenable course? Perhaps we can only speculate. A flagrant display: At one point in a recent seminar discussion I repeated, "Only God can make a tree." And then this exclamation by a graduate student, "Up until now!" This, it appears to me, is the reflection of a notion, so prevalent in the eighteenth and nineteenth centuries, that every facet of Creation, even life itself, lies within the powers of man. Merely a matter of time!

---

[4]For more on the GNP fallacy and how economic growth cannot be "factually" reported, see "A Measure of Growth" in my *Deeper Than You Think* (Irvington-on-Hudson, N.Y.: The Foundation for Economic Education, Inc., 1967), pp. 70-84.

To tear human action asunder and then to assign symbols or labels to the pieces, as the scientists properly do with the chemical elements, is no service to economic understanding. This method makes understanding impossible for the simple reason that it presupposes numerous phases of human action that can be mathematically or scientifically distinguished one from the other when such is not the case. Why am I motivated to write this or you to read it? Doubtless, each of us can render a judgment of sorts but it will not be, cannot be, in the language of science.

Political economy is as easy or, perhaps, as difficult to understand and practice as the Golden Rule or the Ten Commandments. Economics is no more than a study of how scarcity is best overcome, and the first thing we need to realize is that this is accomplished by the continued application of human action to natural resources.

Natural resources are what they are, no more, no less—the ultimate given! The variable is human action.

A Study of Human Action

Political economy, then, resolves itself into the study of what is and what is not intelligent human action. It should attempt to answer such questions as:

Is creative energy more efficiently released among free or coerced men?

Is freedom to choose as much a right of one as another?

Who has the right to the fruits of labor—the producer or nonproducer?

How is value determined—by political authority, cost

of production, or by what others will give in willing exchange?

What actions of men should be restrained—creative actions or only destructive actions?

How dependent is overcoming scarcity on honesty, respect of each for the rights of others, the entrepreneurial spirit, an intelligent interpretation of self-interest?

Viewed in this manner, political economy is not a natural science like chemistry or physics but, rather, a division of moral philosophy—a study of what is right and what is wrong in overcoming scarcity and maximizing prosperity—the problem to which it addresses itself.

Once we drop the "scientific" jargon and begin to study political economy for what it really is, then its mastery ranks in difficulty with understanding that one should never do to others that which he would not have them do unto him.

14 • THE CASE FOR DICTATORSHIP

But methought it lessened my esteem for a king, that he should not be able to command the rain.

—Samuel Pepys

● IT IS MY CONTENTION that the case for dictatorship has never been spelled out clearly, that people generally have fallen under authoritarian rule without knowing what was happening to them, and certainly without careful consideration of the alternative—a free society. I believe the prospects for liberty would be greatly improved if the arguments for dictatorship were better known and considered. These arguments imply a certain reading of human nature and destiny; so first, several fundamental questions must be raised about the nature of man and his purpose.

What are the distinguishing features of the human person, the characteristics which mark off Man as a distinct species? The late Lecomte du Noüy, a devout Christian and also a dintinguished scientist, deals with this question in his *Human Destiny:*

> The negation of free will, the negation of moral responsibility; the individual considered merely as a physico-chemical unit, as a particle of living matter, hardly different from the other animals, inevitably brings about the death of moral man, the suppression of all spirituality, of all hope, the frightful and discouraging feeling of total uselessness.
>
> Now, what characterizes man, *as Man,* is precisely the presence in him of abstract ideas, of moral ideas, of spiritual ideas, and it is only of these that he can be proud.
>
> It must be demonstrated that every man has a part to play and that *he is free to play it or not; . . .* in brief, human dignity is not a vain word, and that when man is not convinced of this and does not try to attain this dignity, he lowers himself to the level of the beast.[1]

This author affirms a belief held by numerous people, namely, that man is a creation of God and is distinguished from other creatures by free will, a freedom so pronounced that he can stultify himself by denying his Maker. That is to say, when man is not convinced of himself *as Man,* as in this relationship to a spiritual principle, and as endowed with this dignity, he "lowers himself to the level of the beast."

If we concede, as du Noüy implies, that the destiny of man is to evolve in awareness, perception, consciousness, we observe that this evolution has been markedly uneven—

---

[1] See *Human Destiny* by Lecomte du Noüy (New York: A Mentor Book, 1947), pp. xiii-xiv.

a few are seers, many are crippled by either inborn or self-induced blindness. Doubtless, there are several ways to account for these fantastic variations. Part of the explanation lies in genealogical phenomena, each of us being the product of weird combinations of ancestors running back to the barbarian. Another, of course, is du Noüy's contention that the philosophy of materialism effectively prevents man from accepting his role *as Man*. In any event, human beings—as we observe them today—are in every conceivable stage of imperfection.

Societal Arrangements Devised by Man

Man, *as Man*, is one thing; he is a created being with the capacity to choose. Society is quite another matter. The societal situation—good, bad, or indifferent—is not the creation of God but of human beings themselves in their stages of imperfection. This situation—our life in society—is governed by what we are, how far evolved we are, and how we conduct ourselves in relation to each other. Each individual is what he is by reason of what he conceives himself to be and how he employs his faculties; and society is what it is by reason of what we are. Considering the mix that comprises society—ranging from barbarians, morons, "beasts" to the few we call geniuses—a good society is, at best, an aspiration, a situation to be striven for—a rational possibility, perhaps, but hardly a reasoned likelihood. However, it is the striving that counts, constant endeavor being basic to the role of man, *as Man*.

Reviewing history, we observe that societal arrangements fall into two broad categories, neither of which has ever existed—or ever will exist—in pure form. At one pole is the social ideal which stresses the freedom of the individual to choose, that is, to exercise free will. The opposing social scheme arranges that the choosing for each be done by another, that is, by a coercively imposed will. Man *as Man* or man in a master-slave arrangement! Appropriate labels for these two forms of society are freedom and dictatorship.

History also reveals that freedom often has arisen from dictatorial wreckage. Dictatorships, being at odds with human destiny and the nature of man, sooner or later exhaust their bag of tricks and tumble into a shambles. And when they fail and fall, there stands man *as Man*, self-responsible, of necessity, for his overseers have faded into nothingness. In these intervals when man is free are to be found the several miracles that brighten the historical scene— from Athens to America! In none of these instances was freedom a planned or premeditated thing—people simply had it when the dictatorship dissolved. Freedom and self-responsibility are one and the same; this trait flowers and blooms in the decay of authoritarianism. Man does not and cannot construct this bloom, this being beyond his capabilities. All that lies within his potential is to recognize the utter fallacy of dictatorship, always and forever preparing himself for the day when he may be free and self-responsible. Herein lies the role for rationality.

Kinds of Dictatorship

Dictatorship! We do a grave disservice to rational analysis when we think of dictatorship as limited to those arrangements presided over by such celebrated characters as Genghis Khan, Charlemagne, Mussolini, Hitler, Stalin, and the like. Rarely, if ever, has freedom been more snuffed out than in today's Uruguay—democratic to the core.[2] Observe that this is no one-man dictatorship but a majority-vote monstrosity. Democracy can be, and often is, far more tyrannical than Spain's Franco, for instance. To view our problem realistically, we must begin with a precise definition of dictatorship.

Here is mine: Dictatorship is equivalent to the state ownership and control of the *means* of production (government planning of the economy) and/or the state ownership and control of the *results* of production (government welfarism). In a word, life control!

When we analyze societal situations with this definition in mind fascism cannot be distinguished from nazism, communism, Fabianism, socialism, the planned economy, or the welfare state—except in terms of window dressing. Actually, no distinction is warranted. The political or societal situation is dictatorial to the extent that the definition applies.

When we "call a spade a spade," as this definition permits us to do, we discover a considerable dictatorship going on right here at home, the clever phrasing and pretty labeling by the social theorists and politicians to the contrary notwithstanding. If one cannot grow all the wheat he pleases on his own land, what matters it if the taboo be called "communism" as in Russia, or "the farm program"

---

[2] See "A Lesson from Uruguay" by Dr. Howard E. Kershner, *The Freeman*, June, 1964, and "Uruguay: Welfare State Gone Wild" by Henry Hazlitt, *The Freeman*, April, 1969.

as in the U.S.A.? Creativity is dictatorially suppressed both here and there. Thousands of such shocking comparisons come to light when the right definition is used. Dictatorship all over the place!

The case for freedom has been honestly and studiously attempted by a few persons in every age throughout recorded history—from Urukagina in ancient Lagash to this very moment when untold numbers of persons are putting their minds to it. The fact that no one has more than scratched the surface has an explanation, a point I shall comment on later.

If Only I Were in Charge . . .

But, to my knowledge, a coherent case for dictatorship has never been made. Yes, excuses galore, ranging from "I am doing this for their own good" to such nonsense as "government [as the] quarterback of the economy."[3] Why has the real case for dictatorship never been made? Either those of an authoritarian mentality are incapable of grasping their own case or, if capable, unable to stomach it. Certainly, unwilling to proclaim it! So, let me state their case as clearly as I can.

More than forty years ago the young editor of a metropolitan newspaper said to me in all seriousness, "Were I in charge of the American economy, all of us would fare better than now!" From that day forward I have made it a point to watch for signs of this type of mentality, often re-

---

[3]See *The New York Times Book Review,* May 30, 1971, p. 11. See also Chapter 15.

vealed inadvertently in innocent utterances or writings or actions.

Interestingly enough, this trait reveals itself in every walk of life and is so common that it appears to be instinctive, dominating unless downed by reason and self-discipline or by the kind of wisdom that lies in knowing one knows not. It shows up in charwomen no less than in those who have the reigns of government in hand, no less in the untutored than among the prestigiously educated. The only difference in this respect is the coercive power or the stunning prestige to lord it over others, to implement the little-god impulse.

To make the case for dictatorship, let me put myself in a typical dictator's shoes—domestic or foreign variety—and make his argument as it should be made. Here goes:

Dealing with Humanity at Large

True, I have given up any thought of managing my wife and, instead, let her manage me. My children on whom I have tried now reprimand, now punishment, now suasion, now reward, do not respond satisfactorily to any method; and no expostulation prevents their mother from treating them in ways I think mischievous. So, too, my dealings with some of those in my employ. Rarely do I succeed for long, whether by reasoning or scolding: the falling short of attention, or punctuality, or cleanliness, or sobriety, leads to constant personal changes. Yet, difficult as I find it to deal with humanity in detail, I am confident of my ability to deal with humanity at large. Citizens, not one-thousandth of whom I know, not one-hundredth of whom I have ever seen, and the great mass of whom belong to classes having habits and modes of thought of which I have but dim notions, will act—I feel sure—as I would have them do.[4]

Further, while I have never really succeeded in any business venture and my personal investment program has been a failure, I entertain no doubts whatsoever that were I in charge of the entire American economy, all the people would fare better than now.

When it comes right down to it, I am more competent to manage your life than you are. I know better than you what you should invent, discover, create, where you should labor and on what terms, and what and with whom you should exchange. Why, I even know how you should be educated, what books you should study, which is to say, what thoughts you should entertain.

You are well advised to forget your personal goals and devote your life to the national goals I am competent to prescribe for the good of all.

If you are more successful than others, I know what fruits of your labor should be taken from you and bestowed on others who are less successful. Rely on me for these dispensations and forget the practice of Judeo-Christian charity. True, I do not know your neighbor, but the statistical data which I know how to compile provides me with information superior to your personal judgments.

I know all about money and how to govern its quantity so as to serve the greatest good for the greatest number.

Forget market pricing as a means of adjusting supply

---

[4]Paraphrased from Herbert Spencer's *Man versus the State* (Caldwell Idaho: The Caxton Printers, Ltd., 1944).

and demand. Leave the decisions about what should be produced and in what quantity to me. For I understand how to keep the economy finely tuned by wage and price controls. And I know how to ration what you should consume.

Frankly, I see everything clearly; even the forces of Creation are not beyond my ken. Indeed, I propose in the not too distant future to control the weather! I need nothing added to my wisdom except the physical power—government—to enforce my ways and to rule out freedom of choice by others.

The foregoing description of the authoritarian mentality calls for a word of caution. Above all, we must be charitable toward the authoritarian. To pronounce him unintelligent is to refute our own thesis, namely, that there is no one who knows overmuch. The common mark of an authoritarian is a blind spot, one that few have ever been able to remedy: not knowing how little he knows. Is a person to be condemned for what he does not yet know? If so, then reflect on how little we know about making the case for freedom. No one has gone beyond the primer level!

So, instead of carping at the little-god syndrome, let us concentrate on overcoming our own inadequacies. Bear in mind Victor Hugo's sage observation: "More powerful than armies is an idea whose time has come." It appears obvious that the time has not yet come for the freedom idea. When? As stated previously, it may be any century now, or decade, or year, or day. Indeed, it may be any hour. Therefore, let us make certain that the idea is as refined as we can make it: polished, shiny, attractive, and ready for eager acceptance. This is the role of man *as Man!*

15 • UNCLE SAM AS QUARTERBACK

I have never been able to conceive how any rational being could propose happiness to himself from the exercise of power over others.

—Jefferson

● CLICHES AND PLAUSIBILITIES critical of and antagonistic to the free market, limited government, private ownership way of life and favorable to governmental takeover of the economy have been on the increase in the United States since the turn of the century. What began in a small way with the scribblings of a few "parlor pinks" has built to a crescendo; it dominates the current consensus, pouring forth almost as much from businessmen as from labor officials, politicians, or modern social theorists. Much of today's talk in the private clubs of the well-to-do differs more in vocabulary than in content from what Leninists were saying sixty years ago.

These countless buzzings of general discontent reflect such an abysmal lack of understanding of the respective roles of the free market and of governmental action that their numerous fallacies are difficult to grapple onto and explain. Knock down one and up pop a dozen others with new phrasings—like trying to parry each icy missile in a hail storm!

Social Theorists to the Rescue

But now the social theorists have come to our aid, bringing the whole kit and caboodle of socialistic notions together into this well-exposed target: they advocate a restructuring of society that

> . . . would allow the legitimate government to recapture *its proper role as the quarterback of the economy* . . .[1]

Now, I cannot find any evidence in American history that it was ever the proper role of government to quarterback the economy. It well may be a socialistic aspiration to *capture* that role for government; certainly a situation cannot be *recaptured* if it has never existed.

But, be that as it may, to view government in "its proper role as the quarterback of the economy" puts the whole socialistic thesis in precisely the vulnerable position it deserves. In the first place, this is very loose analogy, at best, as loose as the thesis itself. For a football team presupposes opposition, something to contest against. Obviously, when an economy is socialized, visualized as being quarterbacked, the free economy is nonexistent. The private sector has been liquidated, so there is no opposition—

---

[1]*America, Inc.* by Morton Mintz and Jerry S. Cohen (New York: The Dial Press). See *The New York Times Book Review*, May 30, 1971, p. 11.

the whole thing no more than phantom play. Nonetheless, this is their analogy, not mine. Let's have a look at its further absurdities.

In the backfield is Uncle Sam as quarterback, calling all the plays. And who better at fullback—the powerful line plunger—than Labor! Imagine Agriculture and Industry in the halfback positions; and in the line: Education, Finance, Insurance, Trade, Transportation, Medicine, and Religion. Others are on the bench.

Labor as Player Coach

Before analyzing the competence of Uncle Sam to call all plays, let us reflect on the players in this dream team.

Labor, as popularly conceived, is organized union labor. If this definition be used, than Labor is telling Uncle Sam what plays to call—really the coach! Labor, as thus defined, finds this dream team advantageous, a way of getting its way without giving the appearance of lording it over the economy.

Labor, however, in any meaningful sense, includes everyone who works, be the labor menial, manual, intellectual, spiritual, or whatever. This includes all creative endeavors in their infinite variety from the simplest to the most complex. No man who ever lived has the remotest notion of what all of this is; indeed, no one of us has more than a shallow grasp of his own aptitudes and potentialities. How are we to appraise a fullback who believes he can call all of these plays!

Or, suppose that Uncle Sam as quarterback is to call the play with a handoff to Agriculture, one of the halfbacks.

What super quarterback could even begin to conceive of the problems and potentialities of Agriculture? What about his weight; are there too many farmers? Shall their number be reduced through a crash diet? Or will Agriculture be given a 2-yard, price-support bonus on each plunge—a subsidy to offset the extra weight? And what about the territory between the 30- and the 40-yard line: how can Agriculture cross that distance if it is locked up in the Soil Bank? Is the turf in the proper condition, or does it need fertilizer, or perhaps new seed varieties? And if Agriculture is held out of the play because of the Soil Bank, who is to guard against the Agricultural equivalent on the foreign team who neither understands nor cares about such rules? Shall the sequence of plays be Corn—Oats—Clover, or Corn—Corn—Corn? What if the defense comes up with a plague of locusts or a blight against the Corn play? May DDT be used to spray the pests? What minor trace elements should be added to the soil to perk up the play? And who is going to control the weather to guarantee the solid footing Agriculture needs? How on earth can Uncle Sam as quarterback ever manage the intricacies of an Agriculture influenced by unforeseeable conditions around the world?

Control of All Industry

Consider the other halfback: Industry. Bear in mind that no single person knows how to make so simple a thing as an ordinary wooden lead pencil. Then reflect on the fact that General Electric, for instance, manufactures more than 200,000 separate items, each far more complex than a pencil. No employee of the company knows how to make any one of them; indeed, no employee knows what all the items are. Now, envision the tens of thousands of industries, many of them making products never heard of by you or me or anyone else. Uncle Sam is going to quarterback all of these plays?

Education is at left end by reason of its experience at that position. Under government quarterbacking longer than any other member of the dream team, its performance is now drawing more boos than cheers. The folly of a system of government schooling is so blatant that it should be self-evident to any but its victims. Pick your quarterback, Uncle Sam or Solomon, and observe how farcical it is for him to call the plays for Education—what you should learn or read or think or create—as if the task of Education were to make carbon copies of human beings! Who could have called the plays for Socrates, Michaelangelo, Galileo, Beethoven, Edison, Lincoln? All progress since the dawn of humanity has been due to fortunate escapes from quarterbacking: every discovery, invention, insight, each intuitive experience is the result of the exercise of free will, volition, the spirit of inquiry. In no instance has intellectual, moral, or spiritual progress been masterminded—the plays called— by government as quarterback!

Managed Money

Finance, long under government's thumb, is at left tackle. I am prepared to argue that not more than one person understands money and no one knows who he is. Why this claim? No two monetary theorists agree, therefore, how can more than one be right?[2] Uncle Sam at quarter-back presupposes that he understands money, an absurd presupposition. Nor do we need any theorizing to make this point; merely look at the record—a rapidly deteriorating dollar!

Insurance is at left guard, Uncle Sam increasingly calling the plays: social security, Medicare, insured bank deposits, compulsory liability insurance, unemployment and welfare payments, price supports, and all forms of protectionism such as labor union monopolies, cartels, insured markets, tariffs, embargoes, quotas—in a word, the guaranteed life. Every citizen in the land, regardless of whether he wishes to be insured or not, is subject to one or more of these quar-terbacked schemes. Calling such plays for 200 million in-dividuals is out of the question. So, how is it done? By lumping us into arbitrary categories—the "have nots" vs. the "haves"—according to the principles of "macro econom-ics." And it doesn't work! Merely observe that as the dollar deteriorates, as is now the case, all insurance—private as well as government—progressively loses security value. Look at the Argentine, for instance. Suppose you had bought a paid-up annuity in Buenos Aires thirty years ago, payments to begin in 1972. Present value? Substantially nothing! Quarterbacking on display for all to see! Failure on parade!

Trade is at center, for everything in the economy revolves around exchange. Reflect on the number of your own daily exchanges: conversations, phone calls, all purchases of

---

[2]For an explanation as to why no one person can or ever will under-stand money, see my *Government: An Ideal Concept, op. cit.,* pp. 80-90.

food, clothing, gadgets, light, heat, gas for the car, and so on, many of them automatic and hard to recall. Multiply your exchanges by the nation's population and then add all the exchanges between producers, distributors, foreign suppliers and customers, stock and commodity exchanges, and the daily total runs into the trillions. Who, possibly, has the effrontery to pretend to quarterback this fantastic process of exchange? Uncle Sam, of course, through such devices as wage and price controls, rationing, and the countless other restraints and restrictions against free and willing exchange!

Throttling the Railroads

Transportation is at right guard. Of all major industries, perhaps none has been more closely quarterbacked by Uncle Sam than the railroads.[3] Short of a sharp and early reversal in policy, the railroads face government ownership. The airlines are headed for a similar fate and our maritime position is also being quarterbacked to death. Again, failure on parade!

Medicine plays right tackle on this dream team. Here is a science in which the most advanced practitioners acknowledge how little they know. And for good reason: Many of the therapies and drugs regarded as cures a decade ago have been discarded for better ones, an ongoing progression since Hippocrates. And there is no reason to assume that the future will differ from the past in this re-

---

[3]See *Throttling the Railroads* by Clarence B. Carson (Irvington-on-Hudson, N.Y.: The Foundation for Economic Education, Inc., 1971).

spect—provided that government quarterbacking of Medicine is abandoned. Imagine Uncle Sam trying to call the plays in this complex, little understood, and difficult science!

Here's Religion at right end; how shall the quarterback use it? Well, if history furnishes a clue, government will try to use Religion for political ends. The king cannot rule by force alone; his power needs the enhancement that divine right supplies. This kind of alliance between the temporal and the spiritual is bad on all counts; it invests secular power with a sanction it should not have, and the spiritual life is corrupted as well. With government as quarterback, we remove the wall separating Church and State; we politicalize Religion and we divinize politics. Bad on all counts.

Finally, let us have a look at the quarterback himself, so that we can assess Uncle Sam's competence to run the team. Uncle Sam is government and government is composed of some of the very same persons who comprise society. The quarterback syndrome probably is no more or less prevalent among government personnel than among the rest of the population. The social theorists who argue for Uncle Sam as quarterback or the persons who run to government for succor express as much faith in the power play as do those in government who believe themselves competent to call and execute the plays.

Our present examination, however, is limited to those who call the plays. What is their competence? How are they to be distinguished from ordinary folk like us? What have they got that you and I as citizens do not possess? How all-wise are they?

Although these persons come from the mill run of us, they are to be distinguished in two respects. We can grasp the first by reference to Socrates. That Athenian, generally conceded to be a wise man, was convinced that he knew nothing. *Those who rely on the power play have no such conviction!* Indeed, it is this blindness to their limitations that most prominently brands them. They entertain no doubt whatsoever about their ability to run our lives.

Their second distinguishing feature is the coercive force at their disposal—a constabulary to back them up. They have the power to spread their blindness, to inflict it on us. And this very power corrupts their minuscule understanding. Such people, when observing others goose-stepping to their commands, interpret the obedience as their own wisdom at work. So, by reason of these two distinctions, they are even less competent than the mill run of us, in no wise qualified to be quarterbacks.

If we wish to use the football analogy at all, then think of a free market, private ownership society, featured by voluntarism and competition—contestants, if you please—with Uncle Sam as referee, enforcing a fair field and no favors. This is the only role for Uncle Sam that makes sense.

16 • THE WORRYCRATS

*He has an oar in every man's boat, and a
finger in every pie.*

—Cervantes

• EVEN WHEN GOVERNMENT is limited to cod-
ifying the taboos, invoking a common justice, and keeping
the peace, there is and has to be an operating staff: a bureaucracy, as we call it. Routine procedures of a bureaucracy offer a legal way to administer a police department,
as distinguished from arbitrary rule.[1]

Worrycrats, as I call them, are a special breed of totalitarian bureaucrats who spawn rapidly as society is socialized. These people concern themselves with our health, education, welfare, auto safety, drug intake, diet, and what
have you. Worrycrats today outnumber any other professionals in history, so rapidly have they proliferated.

---

[1]See *Bureaucracy* by Ludwig von Mises (Irvington-on-Hudson, N.Y.:
The Foundation for Economic Education, Inc., 1969).

We might say that theirs is indeed big business, except that the activities of these worrycrats in no way resemble a free market operation. Freedom in transactions has no part in this political procedure. Citizens are coerced to pay these professional worriers whether they want their services or not. A nongovernmental operation of similar nature would be called a racket.

While the worrycrat has never ranked higher in my esteem than any other practitioner of chicanery, it took two successive observations to "turn me on." Driving north on the Merritt Parkway, I observed a brilliantly painted roadway sign: ARE YOU DYING FOR A SMOKE? While designed to discourage smoking at the wheel, it brought to mind the recurrent messages beamed to us by worrycrats.

Perhaps I would have dismissed the thought had I not read in the next morning's paper about the World Health Organization, operating out of Geneva, announcing its plans ". . . to step up its campaign against cigarettes by reducing the world's production of tobacco." How? By getting farmers, the world over, to switch to other crops![2]

Mine is not an argument in favor of smoking or against anyone quitting; whether you smoke or not is none of my business. Rather, I question the propriety of our being coerced to pay worrycrats to worry about us. We worry enough on our own without paying to have our worries multiplied. George Robert Sims wrote a truism:

> For one that big misfortunes slay,
> Ten die of little worries.

---

[2]See *The New York Times,* January 31, 1971, First Section, p. 12.

Unduly Concerned

An experience comes to mind. In 1947 I visited Houston for the first time. There were fifty VIP's at the dinner. Seated next to me was an elderly gentleman. The next noon, he remarked, "Leonard, you were nervous before you spoke and you drank far too much coffee. That's not good for you."

Admitting to both the nervousness and excessive coffee, I suggested—perhaps incorrectly—that, short of accidents, we are born, more or less, with our time tags; that my excesses might make a year or two difference, but why fret about that!

"I never thought of it that way before," said he, "but now that you mention it, here's a piece of evidence in your support. Fifty-some years ago sixteen couples, all in our early twenties, arrived in Houston. We became close friends, and I confess we smoked, drank a lot of coffee, and even some alcohol. We worked hard but we had fun. Then, when we reached forty or thereabouts, all, except myself and one other, began worrying about when they were going to die. Having a fretful eye on reaching a ripe, old age, they quit these things, watched their diet, and otherwise prepared for longevity. You know, all except that other fellow and me have gone to their reward!"

Observe the massive outpourings of the worrycrats—over TV, radio, and in the press—about lung cancer, heart failure, mercury, cranberries, cyclomates, seat belts, groceries, and so on. Unless one sees through all of these unsolicited oral and verbal counsels, he is going to be unnecessarily concerned. It is my contention that tens of millions have had their ordinary fears and worries substantially multiplied by reason of these professional do-gooders. Millions of people who never gave longevity more than a second thought are now worrying about it. Fear and worry are far deadlier menaces than all the things from which the worrycrats pretend to protect us. But before trying to substantiate this point, let us raise a few pertinent questions.

Are these political saviors really concerned about your welfare and mine? Actually, they do not know that you or I exist. Nor will they know when we cease to exist. What, then, is their motivation? The truth is that I know as little about their motivations as they know about what is good or bad for me.

But let us suppose that they *are* worried about you and me. Who are they and what is their competence? Certainly, lovely ladies serve a purpose, but they are not experts when it comes to your welfare or mine. Nor are publicists, propagandists, the folks of Madison Avenue—all of these people who prepare the worry words we hear and read.

Each Is Unique

Or, let us further suppose that these worrycrats are the world's most advanced physicians and scientists. Would they know enough of what is injurious or helpful to you or me to justify forcing this information upon us or frightening us about it? You and I are in no way alike; each individual is unique, extraordinary, different. Were this not the case, my doctor could examine me and apply the same findings to you and all others. Examination of one would suffice for everyone.

As a matter of fact, individuals vary widely. For instance, an associate of mine must strenuously exercise to live. The same exertion by most people would do them in. A late friend of mine passed on at 95. He had observed a rule all his life: never move except when necessary. Similar inactivity for most of us would bring about an early demise. There are drugs which can save your life but would kill me. This is why pharmaceutical houses publish long lists of contraindications for each drug they manufacture.

Dr. Roger Williams, a noted biochemist at the University of Texas, blamed a physician for the death of a patient because he treated her as an average person—when there is no average person! This led Dr. Williams into the study of human variation and resulted in three remarkable books published by the University of Texas Press in Austin: *Free and Unequal* (1953), *The Biochemical Basis of Individuality* (1956), and *You Are Extraordinary* (1967). For a striking example among his findings: some persons can imbibe twenty times as much alcohol as can certain others, and be no more inebriated! As noted in a previous chapter, even "identical twins" are far from identical.

Beyond Man's Competence

I care not who sits behind the worrycrat desk, whether a dullard or an Aristotle. When anyone thus tries to fathom our ills, deficiencies, excesses, he is staring into absolute darkness. Prescribing for and presiding over 200 million distinctive, unique individuals is no more within man's competence than sitting atop the Cosmos and directing the Universe. Contrary to socialist doctrine, we are discrete beings—not a mass, a collective, a lump of dough to be kneaded, baked, and consumed!

Now, what about fears, anxieties, worries? Are they killers? One scarcely needs modern science to find support for the idea that most ills are psychosomatic in origin. Go back well over two millennia and there it is: "As a man thinketh in his heart, so is he."[3]

Here is modern support:

> For instance, a patient whose parents have both died of heart disease will be anxious about his own heart. When then a normal diencephalic response to an emotion causes the heart to beat faster or when gastric distension pushes his heart out of its usual position, he will be inclined to interpret what he feels as the beginning of the disease which killed his parents, thinking that he has inherited a weak heart. At once all his fears cluster like a swarm of angry bees on his heart, a vicious cycle is established and thus anxious cortical supervision may eventually lead to organic lesions. He and his family will then be convinced that he did indeed inherit a weak heart, yet this is not at all true.

The above is taken from *Man's Presumptuous Brain* by A. T. W. Simeons, M.D.[4] This is but one of many illustrations of how death is hastened through fears, anxieties, rage, worries; a physiologic and pathologic process set in motion by a psychosomatic origin. In brief, unless one would speed the process, let him not fear death.

---

[3]*Proverbs* 23:7.

[4]First published in 1961 by E. P. Dutton & Co., New York.

See also *The Stress of Life* by Hans Selye, M.D. (New York: McGraw-Hill Book Co., 1956) and *The Myth of Mental Illness* by Thomas S. Szasz, M.D. (London: Martin Secker & Warburg, Ltd., 1962).

I repeat, the outpourings of the worrycrats tend to multiply our stresses, anxieties, worries; instead of rescuing us from our waywardness, they are literally scaring us to death.

Ideally, there is a role for government with respect to health, education, welfare. That role is to inhibit misrepresentation, fraud, violence, predation, whether by doctors, educators, restaurateurs, pharmaceutical manufacturers, labor unions, or others. No false labels! No coercive impositions on anyone! This is to say that all of us should be prohibited from injuring others. Actions that harm others —not what one does to self—define the limits of the social problem and of governmental scope.

You know yourself better than anyone else does. Better that you turn yourself toward what you think is your advantage than be turned by a worrycrat toward what he thinks is your advantage. You at least know something, whereas he knows nothing of you as an individual.

17 • PERSONAL AND CONFIDENTIAL

Who shall be true to us when we are so un-secret ourselves?

—Shakespeare

• THERE IS AS MUCH FALLACY as wit in the old wheeze, "It isn't that I can't keep a secret; it's the people I tell it to." Why fallacy? It is obvious, in the first place, that I cannot keep a secret or I would not have told it to you; and, secondly, you have less reason to keep my secret than I. Secrets are not among those things that can be kept.

Here is a good rule, learned the hard way, which I shall attempt to substantiate: Never write or speak anything unfit for all on earth to witness. Indeed, insofar as possible, let this apply to one's thoughts as well; for even thoughts have some sort of a communicating wave length. Observed Samuel Smiles:

> . . . there is not an act or *thought* in the life of a human being but carries with it a train of consequences, the end

of which we may never trace. Not one but, to a certain extent, gives color to our own life, and insensibly influences the lives of those about us. The good deed or *thought* will live, even though we may not see it fructify but so will the bad; and no person is so insignificant as to be sure that his example will not do good on the one hand, nor evil on the other.[1] (Italics mine)

Before reflecting on the subtle aspects of secrecy or privacy, such as one's own thoughts, let us touch on the problem in its more obvious forms for this is an old, old matter of common concern. For instance, the writers of The Declaration of Independence made this charge against King George III:

He has erected a multitude of new Offices, and sent hither swarms of Officers to harrass our people. . . .

In a word, nothing was private or confidential.

Fifteen years later in Amendment IV of the Bill of Rights, we find this attempt to secure privacy under our new government:

The right of the people to be secure in their persons, houses, *papers*, and *effects*, against unreasonable seizures, shall not be violated. . . .

How works the U.S.A. protection against unreasonable search and seizure? In 1949 our House of Representatives appointed "the Buchanan Committee," the avowed aim of which was to enact a law to force all organizations such as FEE, regardless of how far removed from political action,

---

[1] See *Self Help* by Samuel Smiles (Philadelphia: Lippincott, 1884), p. 374.

to register as lobbyists. Hearings were held. Prior to my commanded appearance, there were from one to four committee "investigators" here for a whole month, ransacking every file in the place, even copies of "personal and confidential" letters—everything made public property. To refuse them access to every record was to face a Contempt-of-Congress citation and a prison sentence. That's how well the Fourth Amendment now works!

As it turned out, Congressman Buchanan's objective did not weather the hearings. Count one! Count two, however, is what mattered most to me: I learned never to put anything in writing that I would be unwilling for anyone or everyone to read. But even this was only half the lesson!

Private Papers Become Public Property

Here is a later threat to secrecy. Two government colleges that I know of—and perhaps many more—have added an "Archives Department." Prominent or well-known individuals are urgently invited to bequeath their files—"preservation of the notables" is the essence of this appeal. Sounds good on the surface in spite of taxpayer support. Observe how it works: The donor passes on. The spouse or estate, wishing to carry out the donor's good intentions, to aid education, and giving no attention to "weeding out" highly confidential correspondence, ships the files. Into the "archives" they go—public property!

A case in point: The files of a highly energetic and outspoken individual—well known to me—were thus donated. This gentleman was rarely circumspect in how he praised or berated those who agreed or disagreed with his point of view nor were many of those with whom he corresponded. Suppose you had written him a "private and confidential" letter. While you never even dreamed of such a thing, that letter is now public property. This, however, is only part of the story. A student, seeking his Ph.D., made this man's private correspondence the subject of his dissertation. And this same government college granted the student a Ph.D. for nothing more than a second-rate muckraking job. Higher education, no less!

The lesson? Be ever circumspect in writing anyone for you never can know where the letter will end up. Some carelessly expressed thought of yours may provide material for a Doctorate—of philosophy! Another lesson: Never bequeath to any outfit someone else's letters without his expressed consent. To do so is to break faith.

Verbal carelessness is even more risky than the written variety. Here the record is the listener's faulty memory which is less exact than the written word. Each of us finds it difficult accurately to repeat what we ourselves have said. Another will almost surely distort, however innocently, whatever words we spoke and the result may be far from anything we had in mind.

And now to the root of it all. The words we write and speak have their origin in what we think. This is why thought must be as free from carelessness, error, and bitterness as possible. No person can conceal his thoughts; they decorate every word he utters and all his manners. Those who try to give a better impression of themselves than the facts warrant are immediately pegged as "phonies"; they fool no one except the undiscerning.

"As a man thinketh in his heart, so is he." For whatever

a man thinketh in his heart to be kept a secret would require of others a blindness as to how he shows himself. "I can see right through him," is a claim perhaps as true as it is common.

Secrecy is impossible, a myth. Ask the enemy whose code we broke or inquire of our own War Department. And why should we so much prize secrecy? If one's thoughts be of a proper quality, why should we not be pleased, rather than fearful, were all on earth to bear witness?

I will govern my life and my thoughts as if all the world were to see the one and read the other; for what does it signify to make anything a secret to my neighbor, when to God all our privacies are open?

—Seneca

18 • ON PLAGIARISM

There is a difference between imitating a good man and counterfeiting him.

—Franklin

● THE DICTIONARY defines plagiarism: "to take and pass off as one's own (the ideas, writings, etc. of another)." At first blush, the plagiarist appears to be a despicable cad—nothing less than a thief. But perhaps this is too hasty a judgment.

What makes plagiarism a vice is *knowingly* to pass off as one's own the ideas and writings of another, that is, to make a liar of self. For it is easily demonstrable that practically every idea we espouse and pass off as our own is *unknowingly* taken from others. Indeed, were this not the case, that is, were we to traffic exclusively in our own original ideas and writings—ideas never thought of by anyone else before—communication would come to a near halt. A few observations on this point:

- Originality is nothing but judicious imitation. The most original writers borrowed one from another. The instruction we find in books is like fire. We fetch it from our neighbors, kindle it at home, communicate it to others, and it becomes the property of all.

- One couldn't carry on life comfortably without a little blindness to the fact that everything has been said better than we can put it ourselves.

- People are always talking about originality; but what do they mean? As soon as we are born the world begins to work upon us; and this goes on to the end. And, after all, what can we call our own except energy, strength, and will? If I could give an account of all that I owe to great predecessors and contemporaries, there would be but a small balance in my favor.

- Originality is simply a pair of fresh eyes.

- If we can advance propositions both true and new, these are our own by right of discovery; and if we can repeat what is old, more briefly and brightly than others, this also becomes our own, by right of conquest.

- It is almost impossible for anyone who reads much, and reflects a good deal, to be able, on every occasion, to determine whether a thought was another's or his own. I have several times quoted sentences out of my own writings, in aid of my own arguments, in conversation, thinking that I was supporting them by some better authority!

- Those writers who lie on the watch for novelty can have little hope of greatness; for great things cannot have excaped former observation.

- It is not strange that remembered ideas should often take

advantage of the crowd of thoughts and smuggle themselves in as original. Honest thinkers are always stealing unconsciously from each other. Our minds are full of waifs and estrays which we think our own. Innocent plagiarism turns up everywhere. Literature is full of coincidences. There are thoughts always abroad in the air which it takes more wit to avoid than to hit upon.

● Plagiarists have, at least, the merit of preservation.

The background of these nine observations has an interesting instruction for us. Upon deciding to explore this topic, I turned to *The Dictionary of Thought*, selecting the quotations which more or less squared with my own thinking on originality and plagiarism, opinions I believed to have been more or less my own. Not one of these observations am I aware of having read before. Now, had I not discovered what others had written and had I put these same thoughts in my own phrasing, I would have been *unknowingly* taking from others. Not a thing wrong with that—nothing, whatsoever; it would have had "at least the merit of preservation." On the other hand, suppose that after discovering these observations I had used the exact phrasing and claimed them as my own! What a liar! Such a tactic would have done no harm to those authors who live only in our memory[1] and no offense to my readers. *Just self-injury!*

Finding the original of a given idea probably is not pos-

---

[1]These authors in the order of the quotations: Voltaire (1694-1778), George Eliot (1819-1880), Goethe (1749-1832), T. W. Higginson (1823-1911), Caleb Colton (1780-1832), Lawrence Sterne (1713-1768), Samuel Johnson (1709-1784), O. W. Holmes (1809-1894), Disraeli (1804-1881).

sible. For instance, in October 1970 a book of mine was published entitled *Talking to Myself*. Some months later, the celebrated Pearl Bailey's *Talking to Myself* was announced. It is a reasonable certainty that neither of us took the title from the other; it simply occurred to both of us at the same time. Such is the synchronistic nature of ideas— occurring to different minds simultaneously. The record is studded with examples. The Swiss psychiatrist, Carl Jung, wrote a book on this phenomenon: *Synchronicity*.

Equally phenomenal is the way in which ideas develop. We hear or read an idea new to us. It insinuates itself into the subconscious or some womb of the mind, goes through a period of gestation for days, weeks, or years and, if it does not die in embryo, emerges as one's very own—an "original." I have been able to identify such "originals" in my own experience, the gestation periods ranging from six months to thirty years.[2]

There is, in fact, no way to fasten ownership claims to an idea, which is spiritual, as we do with material things—copyright laws and legal jargon to the contrary notwithstanding. Might as well try to draw property lines around a cloud or a wish or a dream or Creation. Ideas are forever in a state of fusion and/or flux and they defy any precise earmarking.

One might conclude that this evaluation is at odds with the free market, private ownership way of life which, of course, lays stress on the profit motive—and, quite properly. This, however, is to gloss over the fact that there are two kinds of profit: psychic and monetary, the former being no

---

[2]See my chapter, "Patience! It's Brighter Than You Think," in *Talking to Myself*, *op. cit.*, pp. 156-161.

less a motivator of creative action than the latter. And no less rewarding!

Robert Louis Stevenson gave us this aphorism: "I take my milk from many cows but I make my own butter." And I do precisely the same, my "butter" being a nonprescriptive philosophy: no man-concocted restraints against the release of creative energy.

Do I resent the taking and using of my ideas by others? To the contrary, the more others adopt them the greater is my satisfaction: psychic profit. Suppose my ideas on liberty were so widely accepted by others that freedom might prevail as our way of life. I would prefer this above all the dollars in Christendom. And as for credit, I couldn't care less. Personal fame is of small consequence in contrast with individual liberty and equal opportunity for all, even from the standpoint of pure self-interest. I fare well precisely because others do.

And speaking of fare, one of my hobbies is cooking. I have taken my milk from many cows—culinary artists—but now and then "ad lib," adding a spice or herb or a touch of this and that which imparts gastronomic novelty. When an appreciative guest expresses a desire for the recipe, it is given with the greatest of pleasure; never withheld as my monopoly. First, there is a psychic profit in this giving, sufficient unto itself. And, second, should I dine at that other person's table, his or her best fare will be served to me.

The same principle of exchange and sharing elevates ideas just as it improves the quality of food. The more I share ideas with others, the more and better are my own, and the better are the ones offered to me. This is the process of putting the best foot forward.

Ideas come from we know not where; they are of a spiritual nature. When we receive and understand them they are ours or, perhaps, it would be more accurate to say we are theirs. In any event, good ideas are not to be put in storage but are to be shared—as freely given as received.

19 • SPEAK FOR YOURSELF, JOHN

Reform must come from within, not from without. You cannot legislate virtue.
—Cardinal Gibbons

● MILLIONS OF AMERICANS realize that our politico-economic situation is askew. Yet, few are speaking their minds, that is, consulting the conscience and then saying openly and honestly what they truly think. They leave the task of speaking out to organizations and professionals and, by so doing, gain a false sense of discharging their social responsibility. My purpose here is to examine this error.

The limited role of organizations, when delving into politico-economic affairs, is rarely recognized by their supporters and all too seldom by the persons in charge of operations. Unless these limitations are known, such institutions must head down the wrong road—their efforts rendered useless. Happily, the potentialities for usefulness are tremendous, once the limitations are known.

An experience may help to illustrate my thesis. I had been asked to a southern city to lecture to some fifty invited guests. Among them was a brilliant, hard-headed business executive—more or less unfamiliar with our efforts. As the three-hour lecture and discussion session drew to a close, he asked in all sincerity, "I am sympathetic with your philosophy, but what is it you really want?"

My reply: "You!"

Obviously puzzled, he asked, "You mean you are not looking for money?"

"No. This is not essentially a money problem but one of brains—if I may use such loose phrasing."[1]

"Well, you can buy brains with money, can't you?"

"Not the kind I am talking about. The intellectual qualities required to cope with the social problems we have been discussing can no more be coaxed or cajoled into existence by money than can friendship or patriotism."

This executive, dedicated to his own business and typical of countless thousands of highly positioned individuals, is carrying the practice of specialization a bit too far. He has been assuming that the politico-economic waywardness of the U.S.A. can be corrected without him, that organizations can be structured to do the job, that he can give them some financial support, that there is nothing else to it! His only responsibility is check writing.

When financial backers believe this, and when those who establish and operate organizations entertain notions that

---

[1]Of course, organizations have to be financed. I, however, believe no more in "looking" for money than "reaching" for converts. If the work is needed, and well enough done, adequate financing will be volunteered by those who value the efforts.

they are cast in the role of helmsmen to steer the ship of state, the inevitable result is failure. Better that there be neither supporters nor organizations for this wholly unrealistic view of how improvement can be achieved. This assessment is why I replied "You" to the business executive's question. For it is you, whoever you are, not organizations, to whom we must look for solutions to politico-economic problems.

On That Day Began Lies

First, let us recognize what organizations cannot do. My critical conclusion stems from intimate experiences spanning 44 years: secretary of two small chambers of commerce, a decade with the National Chamber, general manager of the country's largest chamber, a brief spell as executive vice-president of the National Industrial Conference Board, and the past 26 years as the operating head of FEE. I have learned about the limitation of organizations the hard way: organizational voices broadcast to the public or at legislatures go pretty much unheeded, claims to the contrary notwithstanding. Might as well howl at the moon.[2]

There is reason aplenty for the indifference and apathy that greets organizational pronouncements. Organizations deigning to deal with the politico-economic realm are typed. They may or may not truly stand for any particular

---

[2]Some readers, observing the enormous influence of labor unions, for instance, may think this conclusion in error. Merely bear in mind that my remarks are directed only to the process of advancing enlightenment, not to the techniques of coercion, violence, warfare. In the latter case, the more troops the more likely is "victory."

interest or doctrine, but they at least pretend to do so. This has been said of FEE no less than of ADA. Fence straddlers or opponents, the ones these eager and misdirected organizations "try to reach," heed them not. Why? Because these organizations are suspected of having an axe to grind!

There is, moreover, a compelling reason why pronouncements ground out by committee procedures—a common organizational feature—deserve no hearing. Having, on one occasion, 200 committees in my organization, leads me to share the harsh criticism leveled at the process by Leo Tolstoy:

> From the day when the first members of councils placed exterior authority higher than interior, that is to say, recognized the decision of men united in councils as more important and more sacred than *reason and conscience;* on that day began the lies that caused the loss of millions of human beings and which continue their unhappy work to the present day.

Reason and conscience originate in and find expression only in and through *you* or other discrete individuals. Committee resolutions or organizational positions, on the other hand, are the outcroppings of men united in council. As a rule, they represent whatever compromises are necessary to gain majority acceptance. These compromises are but stabs in the dark aimed at a position not too disagreeable and, in consequence, they form an amalgam or potpourri substantially divorced from reason and conscience.[3]

---

[3]For a treatise of this, see the chapter, "Appoint a Committee" in my *Anything That's Peaceful* (Irvington-on-Hudson, N.Y.: The Foundation for Economic Education, Inc., 1964), pp. 89-107.

Once we recognize that our social waywardness stands no chance of improvement, let alone correction, unless reason and conscience come to the rescue, and when we see that these qualities of the intellect have their source only in *you*, then it logically follows that *you* must speak for yourself. Not FEE! Not any organization! *YOU!*

Just before I began this treatise, two illuminating examples of *you* in action came to my attention. The first was from a college president, a man of unusual insight and understanding. He sent along an article of his that was about to be published. In this article he had broken his silence on our politico-economic dilemma; this was an honest, forthright expression of his insights and reactions. Integrity glowed through every word of it! Here we have reason and conscience applied—worth more than all the committee resolutions ever written. Who knows! Perhaps others will follow his exemplary conduct. If they do, we will witness a turn toward a sound economy.

The second has to do with a cliche that has been thrown in our face for the past 40 years· "If socialism is so bad, as you folks claim, why does it work so effectively in Sweden?" We have known all the time that socialism has never worked in Sweden; indeed, we know that it can never work anywhere. But try to prove it! It took a *you* to do it, in this instance an individual on the other side of the ideological fence. The celebrated Swedish socialist, Gunnar Myrdal, remarked, "The organized welfare state has gone mad."[4]

Suppose FEE had been on TV all of these years and had

---

[4] See "White Collar Strike Forces Swedes to Question Welfare State's Future" (*The New York Times*, February 26, 1971), p. 3.

repeatedly broadcast these very words. Effect? Probably the opposite of that desired. But let the renowned Dr. Myrdal make the acknowlegment and we can cite an authority on how Swedish socialism is not working.

Having, at least to my satisfaction, settled upon *you* with your reason and conscience as the sole source of any effective change for the better, it is plain why we at FEE have, over the years, turned a deaf ear to the countless pleas publicly to speak for you. Over and over again: go on TV, speak over the radio, get your works in the *Reader's Digest*, sell the masses, reform the heretics, set the politicians right, and so on! And we say in reply, "Speak for yourself, John!"

Well, where does this kind of an attitude leave FEE? What remains for us to do? Actually, a task bigger than we can ever adequately perform, a field with possibilities and challenges unlimited. What can that be? *Rendering a service to YOU!*

Division of labor—specialization—does, in fact, apply here but caution must be exercised lest personal responsibility be lost in some subdivision. Responsibility for a society featuring freedom of choice—freedom to create, to produce, to exchange, the right to the fruits of one's own labor, limited government, along with moral and spiritual antecedents—can no more appropriately be delegated than can responsibility for self. Your society is no less your problem than is your own life and welfare, thus your social responsibility can be discharged only by thinking for self and speaking for self. The requirement, I repeat, is you!

What goes on in society—good, bad, or indifferent—has its origin in you. It follows that you must assume responsibilities for whatever delegating is done. What sort of thing can you appropriately assign to others? Not your thinking —which is nontransferable—nor your speaking—which should reflect your convictions. Such assignment is alienation, a divorcement from one's own responsibilities. What then? Not you or I or anyone else can ever go it alone in the freedom philosophy, for it is as broad as wisdom and deep as understanding. Thus, every one of us requires helpers. It is therefore appropriate to delegate to others such chores as befits one's own requirements: the gathering of facts and ideas, searching for the best there is in ideals and moral goals, and related aids. In a word, it is the leg work, as we say, that can appropriately be delegated, as when one selects a tutor or teacher.

The Role of FEE

FEE's role is of this sort, that is, FEE is not an institutional spokesman nor an organization trying to "reach" anyone. Rather, ours is, one might say, no more than an agency offering such services as you may think of value in your own search and personal growth. This and nothing more!

Once we who labor within such institutional frameworks realize our humble place in the total scheme of things, then countless potentialities burst into view. The opportunities for achievement can now be seen as limitless which is by way of saying that the pursuit of excellence is a road without end. Instead of playing the utterly futile game of trying to "reach" others, we can concentrate on getting enough into our own mentalities and improving our services to the point where others will reach for us. And, by the way, we have a fair means of measuring how well we are doing: the extent to which we can, at any given time, look up to those who once looked up to us. The excellence of a teacher can be judged by the students who finally excel him. You find it useful to reach for us now and, who knows, we may soon be reaching for you!

All of this is more than likely when enough individuals heed the admonition, "Speak for yourself, John."

20 • EDUCATION, THE FREE MARKET WAY

All educators belong in a candle-lighting contest; all students seekers after light.

● "WE DO NOT KNOW what is happening to us," observed Ortega, "and that is precisely what is happening to us." It has always been thus, but why? Let us examine our area of concern: the individual in society.

Broadly speaking, there are two opposed societal arrangements:

1. The authoritarian, collectivistic, all-out government, martial law arrangement, preponderant throughout history and best exemplified today by the U.S.S.R.
2. The cooperative and voluntaristic arrangement that *was* temporarily approximated in the U.S.A., namely, the free market, private ownership, limited government way of life.

One of the things that is happening to us is a relapse into martial law, and primarily because we do not understand or trust the voluntaristic market process. Today, the free market arrangement and its enormous potentialities are substantially in the realm of the unknown. We must, at the very least, be convinced of freedom's efficacy before we can even hope to cope with what is happening to us.

Generating convictions about freedom is an educational problem which amounts to nothing less than how to explain the unknown.

This, in turn, brings into question the two opposing methods of education: (1) the ever-popular, though compulsory, political way as against (2) the relatively unknown and untried free market way. The former has become traditional and habitual to the point of being instinctive; thus, the case for the latter can be won only by an appeal to reason. Samuel Johnson said, "The chains of habit are generally too small to be felt until they are too strong to be broken." If so, it is high time we at least try to break the habit of compulsory education, for there is abundant evidence that it cannot lead toward freedom.

The Consensus Governs

In political economy it is the consensus that governs—public opinion, as Lincoln observed, is the strongest social force. Improvement in society presupposes that numerous persons—enough to compose an enlightened leadership—have free market convictions. Imagine that only one person has an awareness of a particular truth, otherwise unknown. What must that one person do if enlightenment is to spread? How is the unknown to be explained?

The nature of the problem we face requires knowledge

over and beyond the type that can be forced upon anyone else or acquired by the imitative process, or learned by rote; it is not like knowing the multiplication table, how to repair motors, hoe corn, and so on. The depth of understanding required for faith in freedom demands consciousness in the highest degree; indeed, it demands original thinking in the ideological realm. This is not a question of inventing a new idea, for the only newness of any truth is its initial apprehension by a person; that is to say, no idea is really original except in the sense of its first encounter and mastery by a given person. What does this make of our problem? It is nothing less than how you or I can induce original thinking on the part of another. How, in heaven's name, can this be done?

It may be helpful to explain how it cannot be done. Most of the proposed methods are worthless or downright mischievous, all because so few grasp the nature of the problem! Our own attempts to explain numerous unknowns—the free market, for instance, and how it works wonders—are criticized for being too lengthy and not easy enough to read. Brevity and a grammar-school type of writing are admonished, the height of this folly being, "Why don't you put your stuff in parables as Christ did?" When I asked that correspondent to write a parable, that ended the matter!

Then there are tens of thousands who insist on the political approach—to ram their ideas into the heads of the "dumb masses." A Russian scientist, Pavlov, discovered how to make dogs salivate at will. Many "on our side" try precisely this political technique, that is, to get others to think their way at will. The error? People are not dogs; and salivation cannot be compared to original thinking—which involves an expansion of the consciousness. If there were such magic power, it should have no appeal to anyone who grasps how the free market works. Leave these ignoble devices to the socialists; such methods sometimes succeed in promoting clichés, plausibilities, untruths, but never is original thinking induced in this manner.

The Trouble with Slogans

Take the brevity and simplicity thesis. Presently, I am reading a book for the fifth time and only because the ideas did not come through to me in previous readings. The inclination is to excuse one's blindness by blaming the author for the length of his book or for the complex sentence structure. Yet, an honest examination revealed the words and sentences to be quite simple. Then, I discovered that the length of the book was due to the author's explanation first this way and then that. Why my problem? The ideas were new to me—in the realm of the unknown, beyond my intellectual experiences. I was the problem, trying to become what I am not yet.

But more important, why do I keep returning to this author? What lures me to him? Certainly, he never knew of my existence; that is, he did not have me in mind. He was thinking things through for himself and sharing his thoughts with whoever might be interested. He practiced education via the free market, not the political way.

How, then, does one induce original thinking in another? How introduce him to the unknown? Paradoxical as it may seem, the first step is admitting to a profound truth, namely, *not knowing;* next, by never "zeroing in" on anyone, which is to say, by having no person as a target of one's "wisdom." Ortega said of Socrates that he was the most convinced man who ever trod the earth—convinced that he knew nothing. Bear in mind that seekers after truth have listened to this great Athenian for nearly 24 centuries. Had Socrates resorted to the political brand of education, he would be unknown to us.

A recent confirming experience: Learning that I was to be in New Orleans for a lecture, several studious young men invited me to breakfast with them. Never have I had a more rewarding and interesting 90 minutes—intense, and all in good humor. The next day, shortly after take-off for Chicago, a businessman seated himself on the plane beside me and asked if I were the one who had talked with the young men the morning before. I answered affirmatively and he told of being at the next table and hearing me respond to a question about monetary theory: "There is no more than one who thoroughly understands money and I do not know who he is." Monetary affairs being his business, the man awaited my explanation and confessed to listening in until we adjourned. Rarely have I come upon anyone as favorably impressed as he.

To make my point: suppose I had called on this gentleman intent on *selling* him my ideas, that is, imposing my ideas upon him. Some friends of mine had tried that, he said, and to no avail. What is the message to me from this breakfast incident? What secret is being revealed to me? Here it is: I was unaware of this businessman's existence; he clearly was not the target of any intentions or designs of mine. None of that Pavlov treatment! I was merely thinking out loud with the inquisitive young men. It was when I alluded to *not knowing*—unique perhaps—that he pricked up his ears and listened in, his doors of perception wide open.

As if I needed a confirming lesson to drive this point home, a similar experience took place the next day—a card-carrying "liberal," after listening in, in effect, burned his card and did an about-face!

Humble Faith in Freedom

One of the best thinkers among the many businessmen of my acquaintance said: "I have learned a valuable lesson from you. It is that *I do not have to know* how the free market would deliver mail or how it would conduct other creative activities to be convinced that such jobs would be effectively attended to." Here, again, is this wisdom of humility and faith in freedom knocking at my door for attention.

Most people, including successful businessmen, when asked if mail delivery should be left to government will, after some reflection, reply affirmatively. Why? Because they cannot think how they would deliver mail to millions of people day in and day out. If they cannot figure out how to do it, obviously it cannot be done in the free market! These persons have not yet realized how little they know and how the free market brings forth and utilizes a wisdom unimaginably greater than exists in any discrete individual.

However, when one realizes how little he knows and looks around him at the success of those activities left to the free market, his faith in the voluntary and competitive market process cannot be shaken. He sees plainly that 110 years ago no person could have imagined how to deliver the human voice at the speed of light; indeed, he is convinced that no person on earth knows how it is done today. I do not have to know how Creation works its miracles to be convinced that it does work.

What procedure do these experiences and observations suggest? That is, how can one best induce original thinking in others? The answer: *Concentrate on one's own thinking, never on theirs*—not at all! Why? Because I have not been given the world to save or manage, nor are any of its people wards of mine. My problem is me and this is where the eye should be cast—exclusively! Why this emphasis on self-interest? Because this is to align one's self with reality:

> Each of us is interested in himself whether he wishes it or not, whether he thinks himself important or not, and for the simple reason that each of us is both the subject and the protagonist of his own nontransferable life[1]

Self-interest is served when one looks to his own growth, development, emergence. However, an intelligent attention to personal growth requires of the individual that he *share* his thoughts with those who might wish them. For it is an observed fact that the more one shares his own ideas the more and the higher grade will his own ideas be. The explanation is simple: In sharing, one puts his best foot forward; he refines and expresses his thoughts as best he can. Any time one betters his expression, he enriches the

---

[1]See *Man and Crisis* by José Ortega y Gasset (New York: W. W. Norton & Co., 1962), p. 9.

idea in his own mind. If this practice is not an attention to self-interest, pray tell, what is! Sharing, be it by the spoken or written word. Sharing, as with the young men at breakfast. No target practice this; none of Pavlov. And absolutely oblivious as to who may be listening!

Truly, this is the way—the almost unknown way—to induce others to reach for one's thoughts, to open wide their doors of perception. And the reaching will be encouraged if one is aware of the unknown and frankly acknowledges how little he knows. *On the other hand, if a pre-planned response by listeners be one's intent, regardless of how well concealed it may be, there will be no reaching, only resistance.* This seems to be one of the best-kept secrets of all time. And no one can ever grasp it except as he thinks it through for himself—original thinking.

Another confirmation of the validity of this approach was a remark by one of the young men at the breakfast session as he bade me adieu: "After being admonished by Mr. So-and-So, I felt *compelled* to buy the books he insisted I read; after listening to you [thinking out loud, so to speak], I *wish* to read the books you suggest." From which source does one experience the greatest intellectual intake, a book he is forced to read or one he truly desires to read?

How perfectly can I practice these seemingly inadvertent lessons which are so contrary to my own and nearly everyone else's natural instincts? Frankly, I do not know. I only know that I will try to rely exclusively on free-market methods of education— consumers' choice.

21 • AM I CONSTANTLY CORRECTING?

*That man may safely venture on his way,
who is so guided he cannot stray.*

—Walter Scott

● EVERYTHING THAT HAPPENS—pleasant or un-pleasant—has a lesson to teach, provided instruction is sought in every event. Here is an example of how two words, dropped in more or less idle conversation, convey-ed an important lesson to me.

Having discovered that my new-found friend has a plane of his own, I inquired as to his flying experience. He began by telling about his pilot's license to fly small craft in good weather: VFR (visual flight rules). That, however, was not enough for him; he wished to qualify for the kind of all-weather flying allowed commercial airline pilots. There-fore, as a minimum, he had to obtain an IFR (instrument flight rules) rating.

During the final briefing, prior to the official IFR exam, the instructor explained why he was so intently observing every move: "I am not checking as to whether you are on course or off but only to make absolutely certain that you are scanning those instruments and *constantly correcting.*"

Constantly correcting! That instructor probably had not thought of himself as a philosopher. Yet, it seems to me, he made a profound philosophic point: the discipline required for flying by instruments also applies to living by numerous, basic guidelines. To live the good life requires constant correcting, achieved by a constant and faithful scanning of the guidelines.

Expanded Horizons

Learning to fly within seeing distance of a runway in clear weather is possible for anyone competent to drive a car. But learning to fly long distances over unfamiliar territory, by day or by night, and in all kinds of weather, is quite a different matter. The further one ventures from what can be easily observed, the greater is the chance of error—of getting off course—and the more necessary is constant and skillful correction. Truly, those of a venturesome spirit expand their horizons, provided they observe the rule: constant correction.

Analogous to simple flying is the life of primitive peoples. Not much in the way of correction is required of Kalahari bushmen, for instance; they only forage. These little people have no trouble staying on course for they have few courses to pursue beyond chasing wild animals or finding their way to nature's scant offerings of nuts, roots, herbs, water. At their level of life, there is little, if anything, requiring correction.

However, not everyone has been content with primitive life. Millions, with a somewhat venturesome spirit, have chosen to broaden their horizons. In doing so, they have to strike out into new, unfamiliar, and increasingly complex relationships. And the more they break with simple ways and traditions, the less there is to go by—off "into the wild, blue yonder," as an Air Force song has it. They must learn to fly by instruments. The further they venture, the greater the risk of getting off course; each must keep asking himself, "Am I constantly correcting?"

Complex Society Requires Moral Guides

To sustain a complex society we must observe numerous basic guidelines: political, economic, moral-ethical, spiritual.

For example, the Golden Rule is the oldest ethical guideline of distinctive universal character. Many people are capable of abiding by this nonviolence rule in simple relationships or close at home, as we say. But note how difficult it is to practice this basic precept in societies featured by special interest groups: axe-grinding collectives. More and more the tendency is to try to rule over others rather than to respect and treat them justly.

Only the individual has combined powers of reason and self-control by which to refrain from doing to others that which he would not have another do unto him. Such personal attention to responsibility tends to be lost when individuals are absorbed into special interest groups; these collectives have no perceptual powers, none whatsoever!

How did we stray so disastrously off course and wander

into this special interest, collectivistic situation in the first place? Quite simple! Individuals—millions of them—failed *constantly to correct* their moral and eithical positions as they ventured toward expanding horizons. By taking their eyes off one of the most important guidelines, they surrendered their individuality and lost themselves in the numerous collectives. A collective can no more practice the Golden Rule than it can think, and the same is true of persons who allow themselves to become collectivized.

There are other guidelines on the societal instrument panel which must be scrupulously heeded if we would stay on course. Among them are the Ten Commandments. I shall choose two at random, sufficient to make my point.

Take "Thou shalt not steal" and note how easy it is to stray off course unless one is constantly correcting. How many among us will personally rob another? Perhaps one in ten thousand! The vast majority of us would starve before snatching another's purse. Personal observance of this Commandment is so much a part of our heritage that honest behavior is little more than doing what comes naturally. And who will contend that it should be otherwise? Such a person can hardly be found; nearly everyone believes that this is a good guideline.

Collectively Irresponsible

But observe what has happened to these "honest" millions, the ones in the United States. The vast majority who would not snatch a purse to gain a few dollars will now advocate schemes taking not less than $150 billion annually. They will take a substantial part of each other's income and capital and do so without the slightest qualm. Most of them, as they feather their own nests at the expense of others, will think of these actions as righteous rather than sinful. Why so far off course?

First, is the depersonalization of the action; the taking is not done on anyone's personal responsibility but in the name of some so-called social good or group. Second, this taking has been legalized which, to nonthinkers, makes the action seem all right. And, third, these people apparently have had no instructor who said, "I am not checking as to whether you are on course or off but only to make absolutely certain that you are constantly correcting." They have taken their eye off the instrument panel—off this guideline—and are now so far into "the wild, blue yonder" that they regard taking each other's substance as benevolence. Petty thievery they reject; coercive taking from each other on the grand scale they accept. "Thou shalt not steal" has become a mere Biblical tag line instead of a hazard-avoiding guideline.

What about "Thou shalt not kill"? No need to labor the answer, for to do so would be a repetition of the stealing explanation. Few, indeed, would personally commit murder, any more than a wolf will kill his kind.[1] Yet, people in the most "advanced" nations will engage in mass slaughter and, if proficient enough, receive medals for so doing! And for precisely the same reasons that they steal from each other on the grand scale: failure to look to this guide-

---

[1]See "Morals and Weapons," the final chapter in *King Solomon's Ring* by Konrad Z. Lorenz who, according to Julian Huxley, is "one of the outstanding naturalists of our times." In paperback (New York: Thomas Y. Crowell Co., 1961).

line on the societal instrument panel and *constantly correct*. That most people from all walks of life really believe in this Commandment as a correct guideline is attested to by their strict observance of it in personal relationships.

Let us now refer to one among numerous economic guidelines: If exchange is voluntary, everybody gains; otherwise, one man's gain is another's loss. Behind this remarkable guideline lies the subjective theory of value. This was no invention but a discovery. Carl Menger (1870) merely observed how people behave among themselves when free to act voluntarily. What he discovered is as simple as the Golden Rule: The value of any good or service is whatever another or others will give in willing exchange. If I swap two hours of my labor for your goose, the value of my labor is your goose and the value of your goose is my labor. Observe that each of us, subjectively, that is, in our respective judgments, gains by the exchange. I value the goose more than my labor and you value my labor more than your goose or we would not trade one for the other. Even a child can understand this basic economic guideline if it is explained correctly.

The Function of Market Prices

The free market of voluntary exchanges, based on each person's judgment or choice of values, affords the pricing information each participant needs to tell him instantly what is relatively scarce or relatively abundant, whether to consume or to save, to buy or to sell, to produce more or less of this or that—market price guidelines for constant correcting.

Today, millions of exchanges are not willingly but coercively made. Samples: The part I have been forced to pay for the Gateway Arch, urban renewal, and "full employment" projects, going to the moon, and so on. Reflect on the unwilling exchanges labor unions coercively exact from their own members as well as employers. The individual's judgment of value and desire to trade are disregarded. Exchanges are unwillingly effected. This is a substitution of warlike, antagonistic relationships for the peaceful, harmonious ways of the free market. This sort of exchange can no more persist or survive than can a society of thieves. Such a dog-eat-dog arrangement has to spell disaster.

Why this economic nonsense? We have been staring into "the wild, blue yonder" and failing to heed this and other simple guidelines on the societal instrument panel. Ours is a miserable record because we are not constantly correcting.

Into the Unknown

Finally, it makes little difference what aspect of life one examines; the further we venture from the ordinary, the traditional, the habitual, the greater the risk of losing our way.

Take my own case, for instance. I have been delving into the free market, private ownership, limited government way of life, along with its moral and spiritual antecedents for four decades and the more I probe the easier it is to get off course. As one explores the wonderful potentialities of the free society, the further one departs in his thinking from the socialistic world in which we live. It gets pretty misty up here in the ivory tower—the ideal—and unless one is constantly correcting, that is, forever referring to the societal instrument panel with its accurate guidelines, one is hopelessly lost.

If we would edge our way out of the political interventionist hodgepodge in which we presently find ourselves, we need to heed the basic guidelines. The way we live our lives at the personal level is demonstration enough that we believe in the accuracy of these instruments. So, regardless of how far we venture, now on course and then off, *constantly correct!* This is the way to continuously expand our horizons in safety.

22 • BONDED TO CONSCIENCE *

Nothing is at last sacred but the integrity of your own mind.

—Emerson

● OUR SOCIETY is drifting into all-out statism. Those who would stave off this eventuality must—as a first order of business—develop the quality of personal incorruptibility. And I mean something more by this term than first meets the eye.

Obvious examples of corruption include stealing, bold-faced lying, and the like. Deplorable as these deviations are, they wreak but minor havoc compared to the more subtle corruptions of the intellect and the soul which are seldom publicized or even noted. Or worse yet, they are sometimes noted and applauded!

---

*This article is a slightly revised version of what I said in *Notes from FEE*, May, 1964 under the title "Incorruptibility." It was originally written as a tribute to the late William Book (1898-1965) on the occasion of his retirement after 34 years as the chief executive officer of the Indianapolis Chamber of Commerce.

This deeper or more subtle corruption was suggested to me by a friend's confession, "I am as much corrupted by my loves as by my hates." How difficult it is to find a person who has succeeded in rising above this weakness! Where is the individual who has so freed himself from his affections for or prejudices against persons, parties, creeds that he can utterly disregard these passions and weigh each and every act or proposal or idea strictly on its own merits —regardless of its source? Where is the man who can give an honest yes or no to friend or foe with equal detachment? So rare are such individuals that we may be tempted to conclude that none exists.

However, we must not despair. Some years ago a thought flashed into mind: *There is no such thing as a broken commitment.* Observing that people do go back on their bond, I thought this to be at odds with the facts of life. Later, I began to apprehend its meaning: An unbroken commitment in an ideal context means something more than paying debts, keeping promises, adhering to contracts. A man has a commitment to his own conscience, that is, to Truth as his highest conscience discerns Truth, and every word and deed must be an accurate reflection thereof. No pressure of fame or fortune or love or hate can even tempt such a person to compromise his integrity. At this level of life, there is indeed no broken commitment.

Incorruptibility in its intellectual and moral sense refers to a high order of man and woman—exemplary souls we encounter only occasionally in any walk of life. These rare creatures are people whose moral sensitivity is such that infidelity to conscience is unthinkable—even as stealing money from a child's bank is unthinkable to the mill run of us. People who feel little if any pressure to maintain this bond to conscience are not of this order, although even they may respond to persons who belong to it.

The Remnant

An interesting sidelight on the individual whose prime engagement is with his own conscience and who is not swerved by popularity polls is that he seldom knows who his incorruptible brothers are. They are by their nature— all of them—a quiet lot, each one plugging along in his own way. Albert Jay Nock in his celebrated essay, "Isaiah's Job," speaks of them as The Remnant, and contrasts them to mass man.[1]

At the present moment in history, this order of men must be distressingly small. Note the "respectability" which attends all but the basest forms of corruption. Seekers after office peddle unadulterated hokum in exchange for votes; they sell their souls for political power and become the darlings of the very people on whom their wiles are worked. Business and professional men and women, farmers and workers, through their associations and lobbies, clergymen from their pulpits and teachers before their students shamelessly advocate special privileges: the feathering of the nests of some at the expense of others—and by coercion! And for their efforts, they receive far more pious acclaim than censure. Such are the signs of widespread corruption.

As further evidence of intellectual corruption, reflect on

---

[1] See "Isaiah's Job" in *Essays on Liberty*. Vol. II, *op. cit.*, p. 51.

the growing extent to which excuses are advanced as if they were reasons. Here is an example in the area of my concern—political economy: For some years we put an embargo on certain goods'from China because they were competitive with domestic products. But professing to favor free, competitive enterprise, and hesitating to confess that we were against competition, we corrupted ourselves and offered the excuse that these goods are "red." Caviar from Russia—noncompetitive—is imported by the ton but is just as "red" as a linen tablecloth from China. This type of corruption occurs on an enormous scale, and is shrugged off as "good business." Things would be otherwise if incorruptibility were more common.

Incorruptible Oversouls

If I am not mistaken, several of these rare, incorruptible oversouls have passed my way during these last four decades; one managed a chamber of commerce. Being brought up in that profession, I am quite certain that we, as a tribe, have rung few bells in Heaven. But this individual was different. It cannot be said that he stood out from the rest of us for, to borrow a phrase from a Chinese sage, he operated in "creative quietness." While not standing out, he was outstanding—that is, his position was always dictated by what he believed to be right. This was his integrity.

He consistently, everlastingly sought for the Truth. This was his intelligence.

Furthermore, his integrity and intelligence imparted to him a wisdom few ever attain: a sense of being a man, not a god, and an awareness of his own inability to run the lives of others. This was his humility.

Lastly, he never did to others that which he would not have them do to him. This was his justice.

The city and state in which this man labored—until the time of his retirement—bowed less to the corruptions of our time, in my opinion, than any other city or state in the nation. Why? I can find no reason more persuasive than the simple justice, the admirable humility, the intelligence prayerfully sought and, above all, the incorruptibility of this man. Persons in influential walks of life sought the guidance of this quiet man, confident that his counsel would always be grounded in integrity.

It is an observed fact that many people of oral and mental alacrity try to *stand out*, to get themselves out front, to occupy the limelight. This, however, is not the way to be outstanding. Only unthinking persons—like insects—swarm around such artificial luminaries. As Emerson wrote, "A great man is always willing to be little." Little in the sense of being nothing but one's own best self! These few who live in "creative quietness" never break commitments with their consciences, and they are the ones to whom seekers after light turn for counsel. May their tribe increase!

23 • LITTLE LESSONS
FROM BIG THEMES

*Seek and ye shall find, knock and it shall be
opened unto you.*
—Matthew vii, 7.

● LEARNING — evolving in awareness, consciousness—is achieved by grasping for ideas, thoughts, concepts that are, as we say, over our heads. Reaching beyond what we are is the means by which we try to surpass ourselves, to become what we might be.

For instance, I have been reading for the third or fourth time Ortega's *Meditations On Quixote*.[1] The first perusal was Greek to me, but there remained the nagging notion that enlightenment graced those pages if only I could rise above myself and see it. Only by stretching above my present level could I perceive the author's insights.

This was Ortega's first book (1914). Hardly anyone paid

---

[1]*Meditations On Quixote* by José Ortega y Gasset. (New York: W. W. Norton & Co., 1963).

attention to it: "*I am surprised,*" he wrote, "*that not even those closest to me have the remotest notion of what I have thought and written.*"[2] Sixteen years later he wrote *Revolt of the Masses,* "one of the most famous books of this century, a best seller in a score of languages. . . ."[3] The result? There was a publisher's rush for everything that had ever been written by this obscure Professor of Metaphysics at the University of Madrid. Among the tracts found and printed, or reprinted, was *Meditations*—perhaps the best of all Ortega's writings. There is a simple lesson here.

The lesson? Make certain that what we say or write today will do us honor should, perchance, our works of the present be spotlighted later on for all on earth to witness! Ortega forever prospecting, "struck gold" and focused worldwide attention on what he had previously done. This brought *Meditations* to light, and the book, indeed, passed this test.

While my intention is to dwell on several little lessons learned from Ortega's heroic theme, it is necessary, in pointing out one of the lessons, to quote from Jacques Barzun, another far-seeing scholar for whose thinking I have to reach:

> Intellect deteriorates after every surrender to folly: unless we consciously resist, the nonsense does not pass by us but into us.[4]

---

[2]To avoid confusion, only Ortega's words are italicized throughout this chapter.

[3]*Revolt of the Masses* by José Ortega y Gasset (New York; W.W. Norton & Co., 1932).

[4]*The House of Intellect* by Jacques Barzun (New York: Harper & Bros., 1959), p. 222.

How true, and what a splendid instruction! It reveals the secret of avoiding nonsense. But this is only half of what we need. Fulfillment also requires that we know the secret as to how truth is acquired.

While pondering Barzun's enlightening observation, I came upon this by Ortega: "*Things do not interest us because they do not find in us favorable surfaces on which to be reflected, and it is necessary for us to multiply the facets of our mind so that an infinite number of themes may penetrate it.*" This imagery was almost meaningless until I linked it with Barzun's theme. The secret of how truth is acquired is made clear by putting Ortega's idea into Barzun's format:

> Intellect improves with each interception of truth: unless we consciously try, the truth will not pass into us but will pass us by.

Nonsense is all about us; it is omnipresent in the form of inanities, insanities, shallow notions, often in cleverly phrased plausibilities. Consciously resist its perpetual bombardment or risk becoming the embodiment of nonsense!

Truth is also all about us but instead of having a thrusting or shoving action, as does nonsense, it is elusive, evasive; it has a catch-me-if-you-can quality. Going in quest of truth is the only way one ever can possess it.

This second little lesson is now clear: The acquision of truth, no less than the avoidance of nonsense, demands conscious action. Neither the striving for truth nor the resistance against nonsense are natural traits of man. They must be rationally willed or they do not exist as human qualities.

The Will to Be Oneself

Another lesson: Ortega, observing a *"decrepit Spain,"* or what he refers to as *"a poverty of thought,"* makes the case for heroism and describes the heroes as those who *"refuse to repeat the gestures that custom, tradition, or biological instincts force them to make . . . the hero's will is not that of his ancestors nor of his society, but his own. This will to be oneself is heroism."*

The will to be oneself means, in this context, *"the will to be what one is not yet."* It does not exclude, of course, the wisdom provided by the ages. Ortega affirms this when he writes of Spain, *"Our great men are characterized by an Adam psychology"* and he illustrates this by severely criticizing one of his country's celebrated painters: *"Goya is an Adam—a first man—a man without age or history . . . Goya represents—as does Spain perhaps—a culture without a yesterday, without progression. . . ."* In other words, many of the great men of Spain have cheated themselves by neglecting to study and learn from what has gone before.

The criticism, *"a decrepit Spain,"* might appropriately be leveled at the U.S.A. today. Whether in art, poetry, politics, education, religion, we observe people by the millions "letting themselves go"—Adam men in one sense, with no yesterday, no inheritance of the best that has gone before. Instead of the *"will to be what one is not yet,"* there is an insistence on being no more than the momentary self—no yesterday, no tomorrow—not a nonentity but a fraction!

The lesson? Look to the best there is from the past and present. Upon this foundation build the best there is of self, and then "to thine own self be true," that is, be not swerved by fickle opinions, disagreements, the mores, trends of the time, criticism, applause. To thus venture into the unknown, the untrod, the unreal—fearlessly—is the way to Becoming; this is heroism in its finest sense.

No bed of roses for the hero, however! *"We do not demand justification from those who do not try to step off the beaten track, but we demand it peremptorily from the bold man who does."*

A Lonely Path

Those among us who side with the popular drift or plunge into socialism—the beaten track—are more applauded and elected to office than called to account for spineless conformity. The hero or bold man, on the other hand, often is scorned for his adherence to principles. The lesson? Seek approval by the God of Truth and Righteousness and be content with that and that alone!

"Rancor emanates from a sense of inferiority." What are we to make of that?

All I can make of it is that many people suffer from a sense of inferiority, so rampant are spite and malice. Ortega may have put his finger on the cause: *"There are men who might reach complete fulfillment in a secondary position, but whose eagerness to occupy the forefront destroys all their worth."*

We gain *"complete fulfillment"* only when we recognize our modest place in the total scheme of things and rationally relegate ourselves to that modest place. The mentality which accounts for all authoritarians has its origin in know-it-all-ness, in believing we are graced with a measure of omniscience, resulting in an *"eagerness to occupy the forefront."* In such instances, others see in us less than we think we are and, thus, are unresponsive to our eagerness to be out front. Their rating us below the level of our own arrogance induces a *"sense of inferiority."* An individual with an intelligent humility rarely suffers an inferiority complex.

The lesson? The authoritarian inclinations of any person can be measured by the amount of rancor he displays. Be on guard! But, more important, watch for rancor in self, both overt and covert; it is the signal to overcome one's own arrogance.

It is not my intention here to cover the full scope of Ortega's thinking. I mean only to illustrate how little lessons can be extracted from big themes, that is, how we can gain some fulfillment by reaching beyond ourselves. Here, then, is a concluding observation: *"We know so many things that we do not understand."*

Many of us can recite Say's Law of Markets, or Gresham's Law, or the Golden Rule, or the Ten Commandments. In a sense, we can be said to "know" these economic and ethical guidelines. But how few there are who really understand them!

There are, of course, some things we "know" that we cannot understand, for instance, the Law of Gravitation. No one understands this law any more than we understand electricity or Creation. These, of necessity, fall in the taken-for-granted category. Heed them, and let it go at that.

Other guidelines, however—the kind that can be understood—require more than the mere knowing of them. To

know, "Thou shalt not covet," for instance, is next to meaningless unless it be buttressed with understanding. We have
to understand why covetousness is evil in order to gain an
awareness of its correctives and, thus, cease to covet.
Mere knowing will have us coveting unknowingly.[5]

All sorts of people "know" it is evil to steal and would
never think of stealing personally and directly—not a cent!
Yet, unless they understand why stealing is wrong and how
many ways there are to steal, they will coercively take
enormous amounts from each other—not in their own
names to be sure—but in the name of some collective
"good" to which they are party.

"Knowing" is of little value until it is grounded in understanding. Of all the truths ever known, not a one is mine
until it is born anew and matured in me. It can be mine
only after I have thought it through. Thinking it through is
the very least one must pay for understanding.

All the truths ever known! Rare, indeed, is the discovery
of a brand new truth by anyone. This is why it is so important to look for light not yet within our vision. This is the
sense in which each of us may stand on the shoulders of
giants—glean our little lessons from the cumulative wisdom
of the ages.

---

[5]For my attempt to understand "Thou shalt not covet," see "Count
Your Blessings" in *Accent on the Right* (Irvington-on-Hudson, N.Y.: The
Foundation for Economic Education, Inc., 1968), pp. 52-57.

24 • FOR WANT OF LIGHT

*We lie in the lap of immense intelligence,
which makes us receivers of its truth and
organs of its activity. When we discern justice, when we discern truth, we do nothing
of ourselves, but allow a passage of its
beams.*

—Emerson

● WHY IS THE PRACTICE of freedom dimin-
ishing? On the surface, at least, it appears to be withering
away. Why? Perhaps no one knows all the reasons, but an
important one is that believers are lacking in understanding and defective in exposition. If we look to ourselves or
our acquaintances, it is evident that none of us—when it
comes to expertise in the philosophy of liberty—has enough
candlepower to cast much of a beam. This suggests a basic
need to tie in with the source of light.

Common opinion, even among those who proclaim a
liking for freedom, holds that our only task is to devise
techniques for insinuating our present views into the minds
of others—as if our opinions were wisdom unblemished,
the latest and most enlightened word which could be imparted to others mechanically. Such reform efforts amount

to no more than publicizing the paucity of what we know. And the most likely reaction from others is to correlate the freedom philosophy with our emptiness and decide that they want none of it. We should realize that ideas can never be insinuated into the heads of others, for each person is in charge of his own doors of perception. We who believe in freedom should relinquish forever the baneful habit of trying to make others carbon copies of ourselves.

Inner Reflection

The only methodology consistent with the philosophy of freedom puts the emphasis on inner reflection and self-probing; it avoids efforts to project our views into the minds of others. Assuming studious preparation, that is, constantly drawing on all of the current and past wisdom within our capabilities, individual reflection is the sole source of additional wisdom or enlightenment. And to the extent we brighten our own inner light, we dispel some of the darkness around us. Fortunately, there is nothing whatsoever one can do about the darkness which enshrouds others except to increase his own candlepower. Such are our limitations—and our potentialities. So let us look first and always to our own enlightenment. To expect a general enlightenment in society without any more enlightenment in particular persons is an absurdity.

This simple cause-effect relationship apparently runs counter to instinct, so much is it ignored or resisted. Perhaps the best I can do to clarify my point is to share some personal experiences. Or, to quote one of my favorite philosophers:

We are going to look for a little of that light. You must expect nothing more of course. I can only give what I have. Let others who can do more do their more, as I do my little.

Some fifteen years ago, near the close of a seminar, one of the ladies participating said to me, "I have the impression that whenever you start an article you do not know where you are going." She told me something I had not realized about myself and my way of dealing with problems. Parenthetically, right theories more often than not evolve and are framed after observing practices that give the appearance of being right. In any event, every article I write begins with a problem to which I do not know the answer or an idea I do not know how to explain. Experience teaches that the way to begin is to begin and that concentration—reflection—invariably brushes away some of the cobwebs, resulting in refinement and enlightenment, at least to me if not to others. So, I have developed the habit of making a start without the slightest idea as to where the "thinking through" will take me.

An example among hundreds: A letter from West Pakistan raised the question, "How can one tell whether a nation is experiencing economic growth? I began a reply but got no further than "Dear Mr. Effendi." I did not know how to answer, but I know a challenge! With desk cleared and paper in typewriter, I was confident that a bit of concentration would give me a lead. Within a few minutes:

A nation experiences nothing: only individuals have experiences. So, if we would measure growth or progress, it must be with respect to the individual human being, not a nation.

With that simple breakthrough, ideas flowed in rapid succession, each of them little enlightenments to me. Never has the writing of anything been easier or more rewarding. And at the start, I had no notion where the "thinking through" would take me.[1]

Thinking It Through

It is when we fail to realize that "thinking through"—reflection—is the sole source of light that we serve neither self nor others. Ortega leaves no doubt as to how costly he believes this failure to be:

> The thinking in the void and on credit, thinking something without actually *thinking it through*, is our usual way of thinking. The advantage of the words which offer material support to thought has the disadvantage that they tend to supplant that thought; and if some fine day we should set ourselves to plumb the repertory of our most customary and habitual thoughts, we would find ourselves painfully surprised to discover that *we do not have actual thoughts but merely words for them*, or certain vague images attached to them; so that we have only the checks, and not the actual cash money they pretend to be worth; in short, that intellectually we are like banks in pseudo bankruptcy. Pseudo, because each one lives with his thoughts; and if these are false and empty, he is falsifying his life and swindling himself.[2]

---

[1]My reply appears as Chapter VII, "The Measure of Growth," in *Deeper Than You Think* (Irvington-on-Hudson, N.Y.: The Foundation for Economic Education, Inc., 1967), pp. 70-84.

[2]See *Man and Crisis, op. cit.*, pp. 30-31.

It may now be relevant to ask, why the lady's astute observation? How did she know that I am forever trying to grope my way out of the dark? Frankly, I am not certain, but here is a surmise.

Imagine my priorities reversed: instead of trying to think something through for myself—seeking illumination to guide my own thoughts—suppose that my concentration had been focused on her enlightenment rather than my own. Ideas simply are not generated that way! The eye of the beholder seeks for light, and hopefully glimpses a ray, but it is not in his power to make you see what he sees. What you see is strictly within your power and on your own initiative; you may glimpse a bit of the light but that light cannot see you, precisely as you may apprehend a bit of wisdom but no wisdom knows of you. However, the responding to light presupposes the existence of light, and to see that more light exists is a proper concern of each individual.

I suspect that there is a noticeable distinction between writings that report personal probing and reflection and writings aimed at "working over" others. Further, a connoisseur can doubtless distinguish between serious thinking and "merely words . . . or vague images." The lady must be a connoisseur!

The Personal Appeal

Another observation comes to mind, this one from a graduate student: "Every time I read one of your articles I have the feeling that you are writing to me, personally." Bear in mind that this has no reference to the quality of my writings but only to the feeling that they are personal. Why does self-probing—reflection—leave such an impression when, in fact, my scribblings are impersonal, that is, without a soul on earth in mind, except myself?

This, of course, is not a general impression—far from it. But that there is even one so impressed is revealing; indeed, herein lies a key either unknown or ignored by most of us. I am aware, by reason of some correspondence, that this particular student is a seeker after light. Every individual who is seeking light is in a sense, tuned in to the same wave length. Intellectually—not necessarily in their reception but in their search for light—they are as the Spanish say, *simpatico!*

Self-probing varies enormously in result not only from person to person but also from time to time in any given individual. Exploration quite often results in nothing— "dusters"—but on occasion we "strike oil." Nor do we know why the results so widely vary. The source of light— insight, intuition, invention, the material of genius—is as inexplicable as Creation; indeed, these features are probably tiny phases of Creation manifesting themselves now and then, more or less, through the minds of men.[3]

The Source, inexplicable to be sure, has the effect of a bonding agent for those who try to draw on it, that is, a natural kinship forms among seekers of light; they recognize each other, for their goal is one and the same: Light! When I read Socrates, Epictetus, Ortega, Bastiat, or any other self-prober, I have the feeling that the author is

---

[3]For an interesting and informative commentary on the wonders of the mind, see *Man's Unconquerable Mind* by Gilbert Highet. (New York: Columbia University Press, 1954).

writing to me personally, and it matters not when or where he lived. Obviously, this would not be my reaction if the author had had my faults rather than his own enlightenment in mind. It is our attempt to grope our way out of the dark—looking for light—that establishes the kinship.

To repeat, the practice of freedom is perishing for want of light. As Ortega suggests, "We do not have actual thoughts but merely words for them." Freedom is richly regarded in song and verse but suffers neglect at the level of deep thought. It is all rote and no reflection, like pledging allegiance to the flag or saying prayers "by heart." For example, "the miracle of the market" has never been understood, let alone explained; no one has really demonstrated how and why we can manufacture countless necessities, conveniences, and luxuries without one person on earth knowing how to do a single one of these things. If the practice of freedom is dying on the vine it is because the philosophy has been neglected, and for this we have only ourselves to blame.

The remedy, if there be one, is in self-probing—reflection—the only way to additional light. This assumes, of course, a studious attention to all available wisdom, past and present.

A final point: If these probings of mine have anything to reveal, it is that any improvement in the practice of freedom depends exclusively on those who are seriously in search of light—dedicated to wanting-to-know-it-ness. Think it through and *share* with those who are interested—that's the formula! Have no fear, interested individuals will see one's light—should there be any. Indeed, they will have the feeling that he is writing to them, personally.

25 • WHERE LIES OUR HOPE?

. . . man's freedom opens up to him . . . an opportunity to become that which he can authentically be.

—Karl Jaspers

● THE FREE MARKET, private ownership, limited government way of life—sometimes referred to as capitalism—is wasting away because so few understand its philosophical underpinnings and the prerequisites for its survival. Those interested in reversing this sorry trend are well advised to align themselves with the realities of the situation, so as not to waste energy in futile endeavors but, rather, to concentrate on the possible. Away with the fruitless that the fruitful may be pursued!

Ask a hundred persons what capitalism is and get a hundred different answers, strikingly diverse, if not contradictory, ranging all the way from entrenched privilege and monopoly to an ideal concept of capitalism featured by freedom in transactions, free entry, competition, cooperation, voluntarism, to each his own—in a word, a fair field and no favor. To proclaim oneself in favor of capitalism in today's babble of tongues is to evoke approval from a few and disfavor from the vast majority, so slight is the understanding of the issues involved.

An outstanding reason for this is the assumption that businessmen should be the key spokesmen for capitalism because presumably they are true exemplars and beneficiaries. The fact is that businessmen generally possess moral, ethical, intellectual, and ideological traits as varied as those to be found among students, teachers, politicians, football players, or any other occupational category. To fix upon businessmen as exemplars of freedom would be no more accurate than to classify them as socialists, or fiddlers, or gastronomes. They are a mix of every fault and virtue known to man.

If a businessman is a capitalist in the sense that he upholds the ideal of a market economy, it is not because he is a businessman but, rather, that he is a student who sees through the fallacies of socialism and grasps the efficacy of freedom. Indeed, in the absence of a principled stand for capitalism, those of high energy with a strong desire to achieve and get ahead—entrepreneurs—are forever tempted to use their high positions in a political way to exploit the masses, that is, to become anticapitalists. The exceptions, the entrepreneurs who maintain a principled capitalistic position, are men who have "worked against the grain"— an admirable moral and intellectual achievement. These are men who stand for freedom in spite of being businessmen. And bravo for them!

Professor Benjamin Rogge makes this point and thereby gives a clue as to where our hope lies:

. . . contrary to the popular impression, there is no reason
to expect the businessman to be more committed to the
system of economic freedom than anyone else. Not only
is he *not* the greatest beneficiary of that system—he is
not even the *principal* beneficiary. Again, contrary to
popular impression, it is the "little man," the member of
the masses who, far from being the exploited victim under capitalism, is precisely its principal beneficiary.

During the formative years of FEE, I naively thought
that businessmen favored economic freedom because they
were businessmen, particularly if they ran big businesses.
However, two friends from the big business world divulged
to me that they were not really interested in the freedom
philosophy, being confident that they would emerge top-
side regardless of systems. This shocked me, but they had
a point; men with their drive would be commissars in Russia! They believed they would thrive, relative to others, in
any kind of society, whether totalitarian, protectionist,
or free. And anyone who believes he would be top dog,
whatever the system, lacks any gnawing incentive to fos-
ter capitalism.

Success Breeds Protectionism

The development and survival of man-made institutions
depend upon someone's keen and unremitting desire to understand and sustain them. Without that incentive, actual
or potential, we can forget about freedom. In whom, then,
do we seek for this quality? We look first and foremost to
the "little man"—little only in the sense that he is not a "big
shot!" He is not one of those who, under authoritarian sys-

tems, would have been a feudal lord, mercantilist, lord of the manor, maharajah. Nor, in today's world, is he a commissar, or dictator, or political coercionist, or farm or labor or business monopolist, or high-placed protectionist, or one who thinks he "has it made."

We might describe the beneficiary as one to whom opportunity is still precious, who has not yet lived out his life, and is not ready for a closed system. He prefers to live his own life rather than beg from others or have others begging from him. The beneficiary is the growing man, one who wishes to become what he is not yet. An Abraham Lincoln or the bicycle repairmen, Wilbur and Orville Wright, or a Thomas Alva Edison will suffice as examples.

The man who is still striving to improve himself is by all odds the principal beneficiary of capitalism or, if you prefer, the free market economy. This way of life in America—the nearest approximation to the unrestrained release of creative human energy—accounts for untold millions of us able to reach seventy years of age and to pursue whatever course our uniqueness, abilities, and aspirations suggest. These millions of us, had we entered the world of seven or eight generations ago, would have been short-lived serfs! I repeat, we are the principal beneficiaries of capitalism—not of those practices so grossly misrepresented as capitalism, but of capitalism as it should be understood: the free and open market. So, the recovery of freedom must come from its principal beneficiaries, those who still aim to grow. And they, of course, are to be found at all economic and cultural levels.

However, only when we, the principal beneficiaries of the free market economy, *are aware* of our blessings can we hope to become effective protagonists. For without such awareness, our improved circumstances and opportunities will be attributed to noncauses and we will lack the incentive to reverse the socialistic trend, to learn the principles and restore the practices of freedom and capitalism. Until we see this to be a matter of self-interest, we will lack incentive and there will be no chance for freedom—none, whatsoever!

So, how are we doing? At a minimum, there are several thousand of us—possibly 10,000—with an awareness that we are beneficiaries of freedom and, therefore, with plenty of incentive—a hard core of better quality and quantity than has heretofore attended any major move toward freedom. As the saying goes, we have the makings! Perhaps no more is now required than a refinement of method and particularly a removal of the blindfolds which keep so many of us from seeing the light.

Look to the Individual

The most effective blinder has already been suggested: the bad habit of personifying ideas, linking them to persons or things that can be seen with the eye. Thus we judge capitalism—free market theory, the ideal of voluntarism in transactions—by observing businessmen. Or we form an opinion of capitalism after seeing a disparaging cartoon of a capitalist. John D. Rockefeller, his virtues and vices more or less unknown to any of us, was for years the target of talented muckrakers, and always pictured and caricatured as a capitalist. Thus, capitalism is supposed to be as faulty as the muckrakers made Rockefeller appear to be. The fact is that the person and the concept are no more related than are Joe Doakes and Truth. The former can be seen with the eye, while the latter—as any thought or insight—can only be conceived in the mind. The one is physical, the other spiritual. And it is utter folly to confuse the two!

Fortunately, this blindfold is easily removed, for it is no more than a careless habit that goes away the moment the false correlation is discovered. We may then consider the idea, the concept, of capitalism—free from that distracting error which comes from personifying ideas and stereotyping individuals. The beneficiary then is in a position to see things in a new and revealing light: the free market economy and his self-interest—the aspiration to grow—are consistent and harmonious.

Overlook No One

Not every one of us who qualifies as a beneficiary will clearly see the truth, even when exposed to it. How do we know with whom to share our lights and our findings? We do not know; so the safest procedure is to overlook no one! Even authoritarians have been known to switch. A parable comes to mind.

The man hitched his mule to a cart and announced that he was headed for Jerusalem to see the Savior. Along the way were numerous persons seeking his attention or assistance, and to each he responded: "Sorry, I have no time for you; I am going to Jerusalem to see the Savior." After reaching his destination, he found that he had overlooked the Savior along the road. The moral of this story, and our guideline: Treat each individual, regardless of status, rank, or ideology, with the same humble attention as we would treat the Lord. That will save us from overlooking perhaps the most important person ever to espouse the ways of freedom.

In summary, then, our hope for the good society lies:

1. Among the beneficiaries of capitalism, those who are still seeking growth and open opportunity,
2. But only among those beneficiaries who can clearly evaluate politico-economic concepts and see that the free market economy is consistent with their self-interest; for they alone have the incentive to work in its behalf.

Your role and mine? Keep striving for our own refinement and sharing with anyone—I mean *anyone*—who cares to listen.

26 • A TIME FOR ACTION

Awake, arise, or be forever fall'n.

—Milton

● THE GREATEST OUTBURST of creative energy in mankind's history occurred in the United States and is easily explained: for decades there was comparatively little organized force to obstruct the energy flow—in a word, there was freedom! This, in turn, resulted in an unprecedented affluence, a level of material wealth new to human experience and, thus, presenting problems more difficult than ever before encountered.

Some forty years ago the prescient Ortega saw in the making what now stares us squarely in the face:

. . . The world which surrounds the new man from his birth does not compel him to limit himself in any fashion, it sets up no veto in opposition to him, on the contrary, it incites his appetite, which in principle can increase indefinitely. Now it turns out—and this is most important—

that this world of the XIXth and early XXth centuries not only has the perfections and the completeness which it actually possesses, but furthermore suggests to those who dwell in it the radical assurance that tomorrow it will be still richer, ampler, more perfect, as if it enjoyed a spontaneous, inexhaustible power of increase. Even today, in spite of some signs which are making a tiny breach in that faith, even today, there are few men who doubt that motor cars will in five years' time be more comfortable and cheaper than today. They believe in this as they believe the sun will rise in the morning. The metaphor is an exact one. For, in fact, the common man, finding himself in a world so excellent, technically and socially, believes it has been produced by nature, and never thinks of the personal efforts of highly endowed individuals which the creation of this new world presupposed. Still less will he admit the notion that all these facilities still require the support of certain difficult human virtues, the least failure of which would cause the rapid disappearance of the whole magnificent edifice.[1]

This "new world" is now disappearing and for the very reason Ortega understood so well: the good society is not a thing of nature such as a sunrise; rather, it grows out of the practice of difficult human virtues, the cessation of which must inevitably spell disaster. It is absurd to believe that this excellent new world can continue when the reasons for its existence are falsely ascribed—as generally they are. Might as well believe that man has no reason or will or self-acquired virtues, that we are but the hapless pawns of environmental forces, that societal consequences do not follow from human action.

---

[1] From *Revolt of the Masses* by José Ortega y Gasset, *op. cit.*, pp. 62-63.

Perhaps the word that best sums up this dreadful un-awareness of cause and effect, this intellectual numbness, is *lethargy*. It appears to be not merely nationwide but worldwide, an all-pervasive tendency. Yet, there are signs of a tiny awakening to the realities of our situation. Such political maneuvers as wage and price controls and a cer-tainty of the baneful rationing to follow, and ever so many other out-and-out socialistic steps, serve to sound an alarm heard by an encouraging number. And these hearers are now demanding action.

Before commenting on the type of action our situation requires, let us pause to assess this lethargy and to observe the kind of approval that springs from those millions, here and elsewhere, who do no thinking for themselves. What best lends credence to my own conclusions is the general "whitewashing" that is now being accorded to Communist China. Aside from admission to the UN, I have never seen this sentiment better dramatized than in one of America's most presitigious magazines.[2]

Here is the caption of one photograph:

Life-size figures (right) in a museum within the For-bidden City dwell on the evils of life before the Commu-nist Revolution. Here a grandmother, at left, clutched by the lackey of a greedy landlord, thrusts a hungry baby to another lackey to nurse the landlord's child. After the Communists took power in 1949, *uncounted thousands of landlords were condemned at mass trials and ex-ecuted*.

---

[2]See "Return to Changing China," by Audrey Topping *(National Geographic*, December, 1971).

By way of contrast, we find this passage elsewhere in the article:

> Later Dad told us he had been "wild with excitement," not only at the fireworks display, but also at the sight of the hundreds of thousands of people in T'ien-an Men Square. In them, he said, *he could feel the presence of a new power.*
>
> This is a power no visitor to modern China can fail to discern. *People power. Nearly eight hundred million people all thinking the same thoughts, reading the same books, talking about the same things, wearing similar clothes, living in a similar style.*
>
> There is little room for tolerance or dissent. "Armed with Mao's thought," they believe that nothing is impossible, that they can move mountains with teaspoons, turn deserts into arable land, change the direction of rivers, and harness the tides. *All with people power.* (Italics mine)

Let us not single out the Chinese for criticism. Some of the greatest philosophers of all time have been Chinese: Confucius, Lao Tse, and others. And take note of Hong Kong—98 per cent Chinese—the nearest approach to a free market in the world today! What goes on in China is not a racial phenomenon. It is, instead, a common mass mindlessness coupled with an egomania on the part of a few—the sightless leading the mindless. For that man in the vanguard is as deficient in wisdom as those who follow him. He differs from them only in energy and domineering traits; he does not even know that he is not God; he is an egomaniac. Some, who seem to relish this combination, label it *people power,* a term like democracy with favorable connotations.

Majoritarianism

All history stands witness to the fearfulness of the thing labeled "people power." One need not go back to Charlemagne or to Genghis Kahn for examples. This is as much a modern as an ancient form of societal breakdown. For instance, it happened in France—1789-1799—years of the guillotine, shopkeepers executed for the high prices caused not by them but by the politicians' inflation, and ending in dictatorship: Napoleon![3] More recently we observe precisely this same mass mindlessness with its indiscriminate executions in Russia and Hitler's Germany, countries also distinguished by men of genius.

I am certain that many people in France, Russia, Germany, in their pre-revolutionary days, were exclaiming with assurance, "It can't happen here." As Americans do today, they thought themselves superior enough to be above such calamities. And all because they failed to note the lapse in thinking and the rejection in practice of difficult human virtues. The easy satisfaction of success, comfort, affluence displaced serious thought and hard work. Mindless instead of mindful behavior!

A growing number of Americans are beginning to suspect that this same type of debacle can, indeed, happen here. After all, many of us are from the same stock as those who have suffered the terrors of "people power." Further, they can read the signs: a rapidly growing restraint against the release of creative energy—a shift away from individual

---

[3]See *Fiat Money Inflation in France* by Andrew Dickson White (Irvington-on-Hudson, N.Y.: The Foundation for Economic Education, Inc., 1959).

liberty to a political manipulation of human endeavor. And when that political power rises to a certain pitch, accompanied by the mindlessness which made it possible, then the worst will get on top because only those who have no respect for human life can "make socialism work." Thus, we hear, "This is a time for action!"

In order to decide on the type of action appropriate to our crisis, it is well to bear in mind the nature of "people power." I have never seen it better expressed than in the above-quoted *National Geographic* article: "Nearly eight hundred million people all thinking the same thoughts, reading the same books [Mao's], talking about the same things, wearing similar clothes, living in a similar style." There you have it—human carbon copies.

One By One

Charles Mackay, writing in 1852, pithily summarizes the problem and, at the same time, gives us an accurate clue as to what constitutes appropriate action:

> Men, it has been well said, think in herds; it will be seen that they go mad in herds, *while they only recover their senses slowly and one by one.*[4] (Italics mine)

Once we grasp the reality that this is a one-by-one problem, any useful action turns out to be radically different from the kind which generally occurs to suddenly awakened and frightened people. Their first impulse is to center their attention on the mad herd and, consequently, they

---

[4]See *Extraordinary Popular Delusions and the Madness of Crowds* by Charles Mackay (New York: Noonday Press, 1969), p. xx.

look around for devices that will, as they say, "educate or sell the masses." Might as well try to reason with animals in stampede!

The actions so often demanded may be likened to "a call to arms," to a Paul Revere shouting, "The British are coming." Such action is emotional and physical; it has no more idea content than the pounding of hooves, the waving of arms, the making of noise. It may attract attention, but is of no avail so far as enlightenment is concerned.

Action that enlightens is intellectual and spiritual—it is of the mind and heart. Enlightenment comes exclusively as an intaking process. When we realize that men come to their senses one by one—never a mass affair—then we need only observe how the process works between you and me to determine how it is with others.

Is it not obviously futile for me to try to tamper with your mind? No matter how cleverly I go about it, I cannot insinuate an idea into your consciousness for you are in complete charge of your doors of perception. The educational or eductive approach is the other way around—intaking: you reach for me and then only if I have something you consider worth reaching for. In view of the fact that "it is light that brings forth the eye," my only useful action —even on your behalf—is tending to my own enlightenment.

This is the only really effective action, but ever so many reject it on two counts: (1) too difficult and (2) even if we succeed, few will ever find us out.

The first, of course, is nonsense. Why should it be easier for me to enlighten you, over whom I have no control, than to enlighten myself over whom I do have some control!

The second is fogged in a secret. We know not how it

works, that is, how those few who are trying to recover their senses—searching for light—do in fact find the light. The transmission of ideas is as mysterious as electricity or gravitation. Fret not; the few who are concerned are listening to anything worthwhile, although the proof may not be evident in our lifetime. As a rule the proof comes along after its purveyors have passed on. This fact should lend enchantment to our work, not discouragement.

Finally, were ours a numbers problem—that is, getting all those who are afflicted with the herding instinct to see the light—the case would be hopeless. We need only keep in mind that not even the simplest matters have ever had mass understanding. Always, a few have led the way.

Yes, it is indeed a time for action—"activity of soul," as Aristotle called it.

27 • EMERGENT ENERGY

I am fearfully and wonderfully made.
                    —Psalms cxlvi, 14.

● MEN AND WOMEN alike, with rare excep-
tions, exhibit a distaste for poverty in its numerous forms—
living below the level of others—and will resort to almost
any means to avert it—even to unprincipled means. Some
resort to violence—"mugging," purse snatching, and other
forms of thievery. But millions who frown on overt violence
will also take the property and livelihood of others when
the taking is disguised and depersonalized, that is, when
sanctioned by "democratic action" or "majority vote."
They will run to the governmental trough, siphoning tens
of billions of dollars out of it annually, and think nothing
of it.

Those of us who see no moral and very little economic
distinction between illegal and legal plunder spend a great
deal of time and thought explaining the fallacies of the

latter, with too little success. At best, this is a nonproductive approach: argument after the fact. The fact is that man tends to defend acts he has already committed; reasoning with him, however soundly based, elicits few confessions of error. *Seeing no wrong in what has been done is to see no wrong in its continuance!*

I do not propose abandoning the exposure of fallacies; this at least improves our own thinking and shields us against error. But I believe we also need to probe more deeply into the root of the problem—attack it positively.

Admittedly, I come as an amateur; I am not a psychologist or anatomist or psychiatrist. I know next to nothing about the miraculous human being—but I am fascinated with human behavior as related to freedom and social harmony.

The speculations which follow rest on my assumption that the destiny of man is emergence; that is, the Cosmic Intention is for man to evolve in awareness, perception, consciousness. Put it another way: man, millennia hence, is intended to be superior to man of our time in these respects precisely as we of our time are, by and large, enjoying a higher state of consciousness than did Neanderthal man![1]

---

[1]Speculation, indeed! I feel as the psychologist, the late Abraham Maslow, felt about himself: ". . . the explorer . . . has to be a courageous man, not afraid to stick his neck out, not afraid even to make mistakes . . . he is . . . a kind of gambler who comes to tentative conclusions in the absence of facts and then spends some years trying to find if his hunch was correct. If he has any sense at all, he is of course scared of his own ideas, of his temerity, and is well aware that he is affirming what he cannot prove."

It follows from my first assumption that man has a built-in characteristic, an innate driving force intended to propel him onward and upward. Growth in consciousness as man's destiny would seem implausible were there no power supplied by Creation to achieve it. It is inconceivable that we are intended to grow without any of the means for growth.

An Instinctive Upward Drive

If my supposition be sound, then I contend that there is hidden within us, among countless autonomic urges and directives, a force which I would call "emergent energy," an *instinctive* gift of Creation which in a fundamental and originating sense drives man in an emerging, ascending direction. This emergent energy, assuming its existence, merits reflection as to its nature and purpose, how it may be thwarted to our distress or be harnessed to our advantage.

At the outset, it is necessary to bear in mind that all mammalian vertebrates have, in effect, two brains: the diencephalon and the cortex. It is my thesis, shared by some professionals, that our problem stems from a conflict between the two.[2]

Man's diencephalon—about the size of a stringbean—is in most respects similar to the one in the higher animals. It controls the fantastic, unknown number of *instinctive* activities, the ones that are not consciously willed: breathing, heartbeats, cell production, glandular secretions—you

---

[2]See footnote 4, Chapter 16, p. 120.

name it! Example: startle a wild deer and the diencephalon will instantly direct the adrenal glands to secrete a more than normal amount of adrenaline. Also, the deer will automatically defecate. Everything to give power and agility—for fight or flight! Or, you may blush at the mere utterance of certain words. That blush is not consciously willed; it is, instead, an *instinctive* energy release directed by the diencephalon.

The diencephalon of man, according to my supposition, has a unique *instinctive* thrust not to be found in any other animal: emergent energy. All animals except man appear to have reached their evolutionary maturity; and physically this seems to be true of man. But not intellectually, morally, spiritually. For there is the other part of the brain, the human cortex by which man is slowly gaining in awareness, perception, consciousness. The driving force behind man's growth in consciousness is that singular and distinctive feature of the human diencephalon: *instinctive* emergent energy. It is just as instinctive as are the autonomic directives that cause the blush, cell production, heartbeats, and so on.

This energy varies with the individual, ranging from near zero to some incalculable potential. There is more of this energy in each of us than anyone is likely to tap; so the critical thing is the manner each person chooses to use what he has.

This emergent energy, originating in the human diencephalon, is constantly exerting itself; it has no choice; it is always on the go, as we say. And, if it meets with no obstacles, it will, to the extent of its power, achieve its purpose: growth in awareness, perception, consciousness.

That's my theory on which rest the following suppositions.

If it meets with no obstacles! There's the rub! The very brain it is supposed to expand—the cortex—that center of consciously willed action, more often than not can be likened to an impenetrable rock! The emergent energy, unable to enter, careens off into countless grotesque forms, absurdities, nonsense—enemies of freedom and social harmony.[3]

Warning Signals

How am I to know that I am allowing such emergent energy as I possess to perform its mission? How can I tell if it is careening off? This assessment appears to be easy; merely take note of everything I do which is at odds with my own growth. Here are a few samples, warnings that I am off course:

> trying to reform others—seeking power over another or others—"running off at the mouth"—feathering my own nest at the expense of others—looking for praise rather than truth—unwillingness to stand alone with what I believe to be right—resorting to expediencies—no sense of responsibility for self—rejection of responsibility for things I approve or condone—worry—anger—antagonisms —name-calling—argumentativeness—absence of awe— know-it-all-ness—seeking followers—gloating—coveting— self-pity—and the like.

---

[3]"Yet, what is in us must out; otherwise we may explode at the wrong places or become hopelessly hemmed in by frustrations." See *The Stress of Life* by Hans Selye (New York: McGraw-Hill Book Co., Inc., 1956), p. 269.

I am obliged to examine myself in this respect because nothing is ever gained by telling others not to worry or to overcome a fault. As Dr. Hans Selye writes: "They cannot help it. Here again, the best remedy is deviation, or general stress. By highlighting some other problem, . . . the source of worry becomes less important in proportion. . . . Nothing erases unpleasant thoughts more effectively than conscious concentration on pleasant ones."[4]

What is it I find helpful to highlight? Simply what my own emergent energy is supposed to accomplish: expanding consciousness. The mere recognition of its purpose causes me to concentrate on the positive and to more or less forget the negative side of life. This *instinctive* energy is supposed to expand my mental faculties, the center of which is the cortex. A noted biochemist gives us an interesting sketch of the problem and the hope:

> The normal human brain always contains a greater store of neuroblasts than can possibly develop into neurons during the span of life, and the potentialities of the human cortex are never fully realized. There is a surplus and depending upon physical factors, education, environment, and conscious effort, more or less of the initial store of neuroblasts will develop into mature, functioning neurons. The development of the more plastic and newer tissue of the brain depends to a large extent upon the *conscious efforts* made by the individual. There is every reason to assume that development of cortical functions is promoted by mental activity and that continued mental activity is an important factor in the retention of cortical plasticity into late life. Goethe [and others] are

---

[4]*Ibid.*, p. 268.

among the numerous examples of men whose creative mental activities extended into the years associated with physical decline. There also seem sufficient grounds for the assumption that habitual disuse of these centers results in atrophy or at least brings about a certain mental decline, and examples bearing out this contention are only too numerous.[5]

Admittedly, all of the foregoing is theory. Is it sound theory? I return to Dr. Selye: ". . . the best theory is that which necessitates the minimum amount of assumptions to unite a maximum number of facts . . ."[6]

Prospects for Harmony

The theory I am expounding has only two assumptions and unites most of the facts that make for social harmony. The first assumption is that man's earthly purpose is to grow in awareness, perception, consciousness—an evolution of the cortical faculties. This is an ancient idea. Growth is implicit in "Seek ye first the Kingdom of God"—Truth and Righteousness—man coming more and more to share in Creation. Even though sharing in Creation is seldom believed to be man's destiny and even though there is no proof that it is his destiny, we would be warranted in constructing and accepting such a hypothetical proposition as a means of achieving social harmony. For it is an incontestable fact that were each person bent on his own

---

[5]See *Fearfully and Wonderfully Made* by Renee von Eulenburg-Wiener (New York: The Macmillan Company, 1938), p. 310.

[6]*Op. cit.*, p. 194.

growth there would be no meddlers among us. And in the absence of meddlers there could be no socialism, dictatorships, wars. Maximum harmony!

My second assumption, which grows out of the first, is the existence in everyone of a built-in *instinctive* emergent energy. How can an acorn become a great oak without a built-in power to grow!

Why, we may ask, is so little heed given to this concept of emerging man? There must be many reasons, but here are a few that seem apparent:

1. Although the idea of emergence is an ancient one, many people have never heard of it, and thus have given no thought to it.

2. Most people are lured only by "cash-on-the-barrel-head" prospects. But emergence in consciousness is a slow process which only dimly shows itself, if at all, to those who experience it. There are few "on-the-surface" benefits, and thus it has no attraction for those who demand quick returns. It is the kind of thing which a man cannot observe, any more than he can observe the red marrow of his bones producing billions of red blood cells every hour.

3. People, generally, think of mental growth, no less than physical growth, as concluding with adolescence. "Graduation," "finishing schools," and the like lend credence to this misleading notion. Where earning begins, learning leaves off—or so they seem to believe. People thus deluded are inclined to associate mental growth and stretching of the mind and hatching with discomfort rather than joyousness. Few grasp the real point as did the late C.S. Lewis: "You cannot go on being a good egg forever; you must either hatch or rot."

Finally, how can this emergent energy be harnessed to our advantage? That, I confess, is a challenge. No one can gain anything by telling another not to worry, nor can I gain anything by telling someone else how to harness this *instinctive* emergent energy. It falls in the realm of faith. At best, I can only share with others—if they care to listen —what I have learned from others.

One lesson I have learned is to begin each day with a thoughtful wish or aspiration or prayer—call it what you will: May I make progress at removing those faults of mine which stand as obstacles to those of Thy ways which might possibly be manifested through me.

If one subscribes to my twin assumptions, then nothing more is required than conscious effort, in the certainty that the adventure will be joyous.

28 • THE WORLD'S MOST IMPORTANT PERSON

. . . this whole world is . . . [the] perception of a perceiver, in a word, idea.

—Schopenhauer

• IT'S IMPOSSIBLE, runs the first reaction, to single out the world's most important person. But on second thought one has the answer: That person is you, whoever you are, wherever you may be, or whatever your race, creed, color, or occupation. This is not flattery; it is to remark the obvious, for you are the only person in the world— your world, that is!

In the same sense that "beauty is altogether in the eye of the beholder," so is your world altogether in the eye of you, the beholder. Your world is what you perceive it to be—no more, no less.

If you think of the world as earth, what of earth do you see? Trees, grass, or maybe the soil a plowman scratches? Or mountains, valleys, seas? Or do you perceive the mystery of a sprouting seed shafting itself into outer space?

Or roots drinking of nature's bounty, topped by leaves which, in turn, use solar energy to take food from the atmosphere? There is nothing else to your world beyond the capacity you bring to your acts of perceiving. The world flows into your ken through your particular bottleneck, which you have the power to expand or contract.

If you think of the world as the universe, do you see only twinkling stars, blue skies, and the like? Or do you behold the process of Creation before your very eyes? Radiation? Galaxies racing into an infinite unknown at the speed of light? A mysterious attractive force at work?

If you think of the world as *Old World* and *New World*, what do you behold? Only the celebrities who featured various periods or the wars fought? Or do you perceive the liberating ideas that led from special privilege and the freezing of human energy toward the amazing creativity that flows out of equal opportunity for all? And perhaps the current decadence in ideas and moral scruples that is taking us from the *New* back toward the *Old*? Whatever you behold, this alone defines the boundaries of *your* world. "Knowledge is a mode of being," runs an ancient axiom; what you are defines the limits of what you know.

The idea of my world changed while I was writing the above paragraph as did yours while reading it. Your world and mine are never identical from one moment to the next. I alone inhabit my world, and you yours. The thought, the concept, the idea is the thing, now and forever, and this, like everything else, is in constant motion.

Aged and well supported is the idea that all reality is in the eye of the beholder, that is, reality is circumscribed by each individual's awareness, perception, consciousness, however correct or faulty it may be. Yet, rarely is this concept employed in what may well be its most effective use: thinking our way into a better relationship with others.

Merely bear in mind that there are as many different worlds as there are human beings and that being human obliges one to live not only with his own world but with many of the other worlds as well. These other worlds are as much a part of the infinitely real as yours; isolation is not a viable prospect. It is conceded that these worlds have a record of conflict, clashing, bumping into each other. But perhaps a slight shift in thinking can lessen this destructive tendency; there may well be a rational basis for more tolerance than is generally practiced.

For instance, would I esteem you less yesterday than today because your world was smaller then than now? To the contrary, your world of yesterday spawned today's broadened perception. Do I not more esteem the inventor than his invention, more respect the perceiver of a thought than the thought itself? Is this a valid way of looking at our relationships? I think so; at least I bear no intolerance toward the less perceptive person I was fifty years ago. So, how can I logically be intolerant of, or unhappy with, those who do not see exactly what I behold? Not a soul on earth who does!

The greatest danger to your world or mine is error for "all error has poison at its heart" and "so long as truth is absent, error will have free play."[1] Clearly, such personal and societal solutions as lie within our reach are the truths we perceive. And this is precisely where our respective

---

[1]Schopenhauer.

worlds can meet to our mutual advantage—*provided* we seek every means to grow, including tolerance enough to look into every nook and cranny for truth.

Of course, look to one's peers, sages, seers for truth; but stop not there. Not only from "the mouths of babes" does truth proceed, but on occasion truth flows from those we declare insane. However far that other person's world may seem to be from your own—philosophically, ideologically, religiously, or whatever—be on guard, perhaps, but bend an ear. Truth has a way of seeping through crevices entirely unsuspected. But it is far more likely to enter an open and perceptive mind than one that is closed and intolerant. Indeed, the inquiring mind encourages others to give forth the best that is in them.

By way of example, I have cited in this chapter several quotations from the major work of Arthur Schopenhauer, a philosopher whose world, in numerous respects, is sharply at odds with my own. However, in his works I find many gems—truths to me. To disregard or fail to embrace them because our worlds do not coincide would, indeed, be error; by such intolerance I would shortchange myself, limit my own world.

In any event, you are the world's most important person, and everyone else on earth, whether or not he may realize it, is in need of you at your perceptive best. The enlargement of our respective worlds is the sole means we have of moving toward a more harmonious existence, of cooperating to free, rather than freeze, our perceptions and relationships.

INDEX

prepared by Vernelia A. Crawford

The letter "n" following a figure refers to a footnote.